LOCAL and GLOBAL

CITIZENSHIP

Rewarding Learning

FOR CCEA GCSE LEARNING FOR LIFE AND WORK

Eileen O'Hara
Sue Gallagher

Hodder & Stoughton

A MEMBER OF THE HODDER HEADLINE GROUP

The publishers would like to thank the following individuals, institutions and companies for permission to reproduce copyright illustrations in this book:

p6 Robert Essel NYC/CORBIS; p7tl Arnold Cedric/CORBIS SYGMA, p7bl Tim Graham/CORBIS, p7r Helen Averley/Art Incorporated; p10 Ed Cashi/CORBIS; p13 both Belfast Telegraph Newspapers Ltd; p15t TOPHAM/PA, p15b AP Photo/Will Walker; p29l Earl & Nazima Kowall/CORBIS, p29r Sally A. Morgan/Ecoscene; p30l Roger Ressmeyer/CORBIS, p30r Press Associates; p40 Credit Antoine Serra/In Visu/Corbis; p41 Press Associates; p45 Micheline Pelletier/CORBIS; p48 Jeremy Horner/CORBIS; p49 Amnesty International; p50 NASA; p51 Max Nash/Associated Press; p54l http://cain.ulst.ac.uk/photographs/, p54r PA Photo/EPS; p56 Hulton Getty; p57 Dusan Vranic/Associated Press; p58 Photographic Collection; p66tl Actionplus, p66tr Belfast Telegraph Newspapers, p66bl Tim Thompson/CORBIS, p66br Michael St.Maur Sheil/CORBIS; p69 Elio Ciol/CORBIS; p71 Nigel Dickenson/Still Pictures; p73 various parties; p75t Alan Lewis/Photopress Belfast, p75m, bl & br Press Associates.

Every effort has been made to trace and acknowledge ownership of copyright. The publishers will be glad to make suitable arrangements with any copyright holders whom it has not been possible to contact.

Note about the Internet links in the book. The user should be aware that URLs or web addresses change regularly. Every effort has been made to ensure the accuracy of the URLs provided in this book on going to press. It is inevitable, however, that some will change. It is sometimes possible to find a relocated web page, by just typing in the address of the home page for a website in the URL window of your browser.

Orders: please contact Bookpoint Ltd, 130 Milton Park, Abingdon, Oxon OX14 4SB. Telephone: (44) 01235 827720. Fax: (44) 01235 400454. Lines are open from 9.00 – 6.00, Monday to Saturday, with a 24 hour message answering service. You can also order through our website www.hodderheadline.co.uk.

British Library Cataloguing in Publication Data
A catalogue record for this title is available from the British Library

ISBN 0 340 86915 1

First Published 2004
Impression number   10 9 8 7 6 5 4 3 2 1
Year   2010 2009 2008 2007 2006 2005 2004

Copyright © Eileen O'Hara and Sue Gallagher 2004

Cover photo from Getty images.
Typeset by Fakenham Photosetting Limited, Fakenham, Norfolk.
Printed in Italy for Hodder & Stoughton Educational, a division of Hodder Headline, 338 Euston Road, London NW1 3BH.

Contents

April 11th

introduction

The first section of this book is about 'Diversity and Inclusion'. It explores how an individual's cultural **identity** is expressed in a number of ways, and how although this can enrich a community, it may also pose a number of challenges. It looks at how the identities that each of us possess come from the society in which we live. In particular, it examines the extent of **multiple identities** that exist in the world today and within particular societies. Finally, it looks at ways in which this cultural diversity can be embraced by society.

1. Cultural identity

What do we mean by 'identity'?

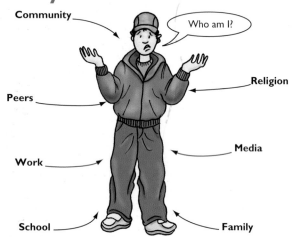

Community — Who am I?

Peers — Religion

Work — Media

School — Family

A person's identity is made up of a mixture of personal experiences and wider images of the world and their place in it. These are provided by schools, the media, work and people who are important to the individual. Identity is usually linked to awareness of gender, race and social status, as well as an image of one's own body.

Identity involves identifying with a particular group. It gives us something in common with a group. It is about who you aspire to be like, and this clearly involves some degree of choice on the part of the individual. Consequently, choosing who you want to be like usually requires that you also choose who you don't want to be like. For example, if you identify with a particular football club, such as Manchester United, you will not identify with all the other clubs in competition with them.

activities

1. Make a list of all the different football clubs which individuals in your class or in Northern Ireland identify with.
2. How do individuals show that they identify with a particular football club?

Different types of identity

When individuals support a particular football club, they are only demonstrating one aspect of identity. There are various other aspects of identity that apply to people, such as:

◆ age
◆ nationality
◆ religious beliefs
◆ ethnic identity
◆ sexual orientation
◆ **gender**.

All of these identities are shared with many other people, not necessarily people you know. For example, at a football match you may feel a strong sense of solidarity (togetherness) with thousands of other fans you don't know, simply because you identify with the same team. Knowing that you share this identity can make it easier to start a conversation with someone.

Do individuals have only one identity?

Cultural identity

Culture is the language, **beliefs**, **values**, **norms**, **customs**, **roles**, knowledge and skills that combine to make up 'the way of life' of a particular society or group of people in a particular society. Culture includes:

◆ the homes we live in
◆ the language we speak
◆ the way we dress
◆ the food we eat
◆ the religious beliefs we have
◆ the system of politics.

Culture has to be learned and much of our early years are taken up with this learning. The identities that we have all come from the society we come from. We live in a society made up of individuals working and living together as groups. None of us live in isolation from each other, we come together to share knowledge, skills and ideas. Each of us is born into a social group, such as male or female, into a country . . . the list is endless. An important function of a social group is to provide an identity for individuals as well as a purpose. Being a member of a social group can engender (make you feel) a great sense of belonging.

activity

Look at the picture below showing some elements of cultural identity. Try to associate the individual elements with a particular group, culture or country.

Different aspects of cultural identity. Can you match them with particular groups?

When doing the activity on page 5, you may have found that you, as an individual, identify with elements of culture associated with another culture or country, such as eating Chinese food. Does this mean that cultural diversity is ending? For example, English is the most commonly used global language and is spoken and understood throughout the world; drinking Coca Cola or eating McDonald's food is also becoming a norm in many parts of the world. However, it would be a sweeping generalisation to assume that cultural diversity is disappearing. Indeed, many cultures try hard to maintain elements of what they view as their distinct cultural identity. For example, the photograph below illustrates how the aboriginal people of Australia have retained their 'identity' and their culture despite the introduction of modern technology.

Aboriginal children using a mobile phone.

It could be said that many cultures and countries try to keep the elements of their traditional cultural identity that they value most and combine them with aspects of other cultures that they want to adapt. It is important when studying cultural identity that we do not assume that our way of doing things is superior to that of others. Each culture must try to be assessed and understood on its own terms and must not be thought of as being better or worse than any other. Avoiding making judgements in this way is called **cultural relativism**.

Using the library, Internet or newspapers, in groups or individually, create a wall display reflecting a particular group in another part of the world today and try to highlight aspects of the group's cultural identity. It should describe or illustrate distinct aspects of the group's cultural identity such as language, food, drink, clothing, sport, family life, etc.

National identity

The identities that we have all come from the society in which we live. Yet there is, in most cases, some degree of choice in the identities which we decide to adopt. For example, supporting a football team usually involves a high degree of choice, although people are **socialised** into supporting a particular team by their family, **peer group** or community.

However, for most of us, national identity involves little choice. Individuals are usually awarded national citizenship and a right to that nation's passport if they are born in that country. Some individuals, though, have a choice. For example, individuals born in Northern Ireland can choose to have an Irish or a British passport. They may choose to identify with either British or Irish nationality. Similarly, individuals in Scotland may identify themselves as either Scottish or British. They may feel both at different times and to different degrees. In this ever-changing world, identities tend to be less rigid than they were 100 years ago, and there would appear to be greater choice for individuals to adopt multiple identities.

Cultural identity in Northern Ireland

When we listen to the radio, watch the television or read the newspaper, we could be forgiven for assuming that there are only two social groups with their own distinct cultural identity living in Northern Ireland – Protestant and Catholic. We do not, however, live in a **bicultural** country (one where there are only two cultural identities); our society includes many other cultures such as Chinese, African, Filipino, etc.

Some of us deny that there are major differences in the cultural identities between the social groups that live in Northern Ireland. Saying 'I'm not into religion' is very common. As a consequence, when we think we are being fair by ignoring cultural differences, we may end up promoting **exclusion** rather than **inclusion** of cultural diversity. By ignoring the differences, we may end up mistreating or ignoring others.

Within Northern Ireland there is a vast array of signs and symbols used to express a group's cultural identity, such as flags and murals. The use of such images can cause a great sense of pride and **social solidarity** for a particular group but it can also arouse conflict in Northern Ireland.

◆ Why do you think this is the case?
◆ Can you describe a time when these images have created both a sense of pride and conflict in Northern Ireland?

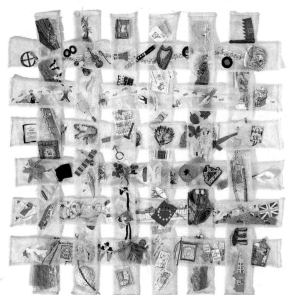

Republican wall mural.

This weave outlines various aspects of cultural identity. It not only highlights the images that separate the two main traditions of Northern Ireland, but also aspects that they have in common, for example, the mobile phone.

Loyalist wall mural.

activities

1. Do you ever display any of the symbols in the weave above? Where? When?

2. Do you ever see any of these signs or symbols in your community? Explain your answer.

3. Design a Unionist/Loyalist wall mural and a Nationalist/Republican wall mural.

4. What elements of cultural identity separate each group from others in Northern Ireland? You may want to consider positive or negative aspects associated with each group.

3. What influences cultural identity?

There are a number of different factors that can influence the cultural identity of an individual or group, such as:

- family
- school
- peer group
- religion
- the media
- community.

Family

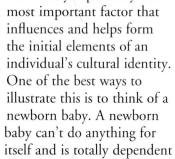

The family is probably the most important factor that influences and helps form the initial elements of an individual's cultural identity. One of the best ways to illustrate this is to think of a newborn baby. A newborn baby can't do anything for itself and is totally dependent

How does your family influence your sense of cultural identity?

on others to provide food and drink and protect it from harm and disease. It is in the family that the child will learn the basic lessons of the way of life of the particular society that it has been born into.

We all recognise that children learn how to speak, eat and walk. But children are also learning a lot more. It is sometimes difficult to distinguish between what they are learning as part of their cultural identity and what they are learning in the development of other skills necessary for human survival. For example, children learn about what can and can't be eaten. While all children will learn that you can't eat rocks or glass, there are cultural differences when it comes to eating other things. For example, eating insects in Northern Ireland is not considered the norm whilst in other parts of the world these would be considered tasty snacks.

Children learn by watching and imitating their parents and others. Their behaviour will be praised or corrected depending on what is deemed acceptable.

School

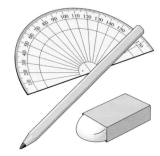

How does your school influence your sense of cultural identity?

Schools are institutions where formal education takes place, for example, learning English, Mathematics and Science. So young people learn the knowledge and skills that their particular society thinks are desirable for them to have to be able to participate fully in society.

Schools also teach us how to get on with both adults and other children, so there are rules about expectations of behaviour – for example, respecting your elders and finding acceptable ways of resolving disputes.

Peer group

How does your peer group influence your sense of cultural identity?

A peer group is a group of people in the same social position who you are with regularly, for example, a group of friends or your form class at school. The peer group can be a very powerful influence on our cultural identity. It can exert very strong pressures on individuals to conform to certain forms of behaviour, especially when they are young. For example, it can influence the way young people dress.

Religion

How does your religion influence your sense of cultural identity?

Religions can provide very strong guidelines for an individual's behaviour and can influence cultural identity. Most children learn about religion at home, at school and at a place of worship and many also practise a religion. Christianity has the Ten Commandments which appear to have been translated into the laws of the land in Britain and Ireland. For example, 'Thou shall not kill', which aims to protect human life, is translated into laws about how we settle disputes, health and safety, and food hygiene. So religion can influence both the law of the land and cultural identity.

Media

How does the media influence your sense of cultural identity?

In today's world, children are aware of the media from an extremely early age. For example, there are television programmes such as the *Tweenies* that are aimed at very young children. Some argue that these programmes are focused primarily at teaching children about their culture and what is expected of them. It is true that even when the messages are not intentional, children will take in information from the media because young children tend to copy what they see. For example, they may copy the different things they see boys and girls doing in a book or television programme.

How does your community influence your sense of cultural identity?

Community

A community is a group of people who share a common identity or a set of values and who often live in the same area, attend the same school, work together and worship together. What makes a community is a shared set of common interests. The common interests of a community provide the people in the community with a common interest in each other.

activities

1. How have each of the factors on pages 8–9 influenced your cultural identity? Think of one example for each.

2. List all the different social groups that you belong to.

3. Copy the table below. For each factor influencing cultural identity, describe the norms, values and beliefs that you have learned from it.

4. Design a wall poster that you think would represent teenage culture in Northern Ireland. What sets teenagers apart from others, for example in terms of fashion, music, sport etc.? You may want the poster to celebrate being young or you may want to illustrate the problems of being young. Consider what your poster will 'say' to others and whether you think you have represented all young people or whether that is possible in Northern Ireland.

	Family	School	Peer group	Religion	Media	Community
Norms (Expected patterns of behaviour)						
Values (Ideas about what is correct and just)						
Beliefs (General feelings or opinions about the world)						

4.   How do conflicts of identity arise?

Importance of cultural identities

Orangemen marching on 12 July.

In Northern Ireland there are clear cultural boundaries between the main traditions that occupy the land. The cultural ideas and expressions are very often seen as mutually exclusive (completely separate) and almost impossible to **reconcile**.

The two main traditions are publicly recognised to be those of Protestant/Unionist and Catholic/Nationalist. It appears that each tradition has tried to establish itself as separate, different and in many ways superior. Many elements or aspects of cultural identities such as language, sport, flags, murals, emblems and music have been established to ensure that the two traditions appear as mutually exclusive cultural identities.

Our cultural identities can be immensely enriching for a country, a community or a social group providing individuals with a deep sense of social solidarity (togetherness), **value consensus** (agreement), **harmony** and **cohesion**. On a positive note, this enrichment can enable us to accept and acknowledge that others may not share our cultural identities. On the reverse side there can also be negative consequences to expressions of cultural identities. For example, when a particular group comes to concentrate obsessively on aspects of cultural identity and give out the view that this tradition is superior, it can lead to conflict. Hitler believed that Germans were racially superior to all other people. The final result of this was **genocide** and the extermination of around six million Jews.

Conflicts of identity in Northern Ireland

Northern Ireland is perceived to have two main cultural identities or traditions. It could be argued that religion is the foundation of this cultural diversity. Throughout the years, many signs and symbols have been established to distinguish both groups. As a consequence we may perceive ourselves as different, for example by using a different language, having allegiance to different flags etc.

Language

The way we speak and the words we use are an expression of who we are and where we come from. In Northern Ireland most people speak the English language. However, the words we choose to use provide some indication of who we are and where we come from. For example, whether we choose to say 'Derry' or 'Londonderry', 'church' or 'chapel' offer clues about who the speaker is.

Can you match the following words to one of the two main traditions in Northern Ireland?

Derry   Ulster   Toicfaidh Ar La
Church   The Province   The Mainland
For God and Ulster   Chapel
Londonderry   The six counties
Patrick William   Craic   Loyalism
Republicanism

activities

1. What is your reaction when you see flags?
2. Are there certain times when you think it is acceptable to fly flags and other times when you feel it is definitely not acceptable?
3. Why do you think other countries' flags are also flown in Northern Ireland, for example, the Israeli and Palestinian flags?

Flags

Flags clearly play an important function in most countries throughout the world today. In the past, each country flew its flag to demonstrate the loyalty and support of the people for their country. This can still be seen today at certain times of the year, such as during major sporting events.

However, in Northern Ireland, because not everyone identifies with the same country, the flying of flags can be a real cause of contention and conflict. For example, on 11 July some Protestants burn the Irish Tricolour to highlight their hatred for the Irish Republic. Similarly, on 8 August some Catholics burn the Union Jack highlighting their hatred for Britain. Both groups have also hotly disputed the flying of flags on government buildings.

It is important to understand that the person flying the flag may do so to illustrate their cultural identity and pride in their country but the person who sees the flag may take it as a challenge to their cultural identity. In 1998 a new flag for Northern Ireland was proposed through the Good Friday Agreement; one that would assimilate both Protestant and Catholic culture. However, many politicians disapproved of the creation of a new flag. Some argued that Northern Ireland is part of the UK and wanted the Union Jack to remain, while others believed that it is part of the Irish Republic so should have the Irish Tricolour.

Marching

Marching has been a continuous aspect of 'the Troubles' throughout the conflict in Northern Ireland. Some view parades as part of their cultural identity, providing them with a sense of pride and belonging. Others perceive them as undermining their particular cultural identity.

Elements of cultural diversity associated with Northern Ireland.

Source A

At this time of year, where I live, the Lambeg rhythms can be heard across the valley. Some neighbours associate them with warm summer evenings sitting outside, listening to see if they can identify particular players, the sons and maybe the grandsons of their contemporaries, who played in the same bands in their youth. Other neighbours detest the drumming and hear menacing stridencies in the beat, and the pounding echoes, which invade their space, spoil their summer evenings. The sound is the same, the message totally different.

© *Contemporary Britain*, B. Ford, Nelson General Studies, 1978

Source B

The erection of 'no-go' signs for Orangemen in the Lower Ormeau Road area (Belfast) is the worst case of narrow-minded, bigoted, sectarian behaviour. It is an offensive attack against our cultural identity ably assisted by Sinn Fein and republicans of that area.

As someone who resided in the Ormeau area (1955–1969) this is only a continuation of ethnic cleansing which in 1968 started as a trickle then as a flood in the early 1970s. An insidious form of ethnic cleansing, where the population of Protestants were intimidated from their homes.

© *Belfast Telegraph*, 28 February 1995

Source C

The Republic's President Mary Robinson has described fears of Unionists about the framework document as very genuine. She said 'the fear of the ground shifting, the fear of take-over, is undermining a sense of identity. If someone tried to undermine our sense of identity, if someone said to us Ireland should join the Commonwealth tomorrow, think of the ripples of fear that would produce . . . if someone said we should join with Britain tomorrow'.

© *Belfast Telegraph*, 28 February 1995

activities

1. Source A suggests that the two main traditions in Northern Ireland view Orange parades from a different perspective.
   a) What are the two main traditions in Northern Ireland?
   b) Consider factors that influence an individual's cultural identity and describe how a young person may develop either a Unionist or Nationalist perspective of Northern Ireland.
   c) Describe the two opposing views on Orange parades suggested in the passage.
2. Apart from parades, identify and explain two other aspects of cultural identity not previously mentioned which can be a source of deep conflict in Northern Ireland.
3. Using Sources B and C, describe in your own words what you have learned about the following terms: sense of identity and ethnic cleansing.

Segregation

As highlighted earlier, cultural identity is expressed in a number of different ways in Northern Ireland. These ways may include common means of expression such as murals, symbols, language, marching, music and political and religious groupings.

In Northern Ireland most Catholics and Protestants live in areas where only one grouping is dominant. For example, in West Belfast there is The Shankill Unionist community and The Falls Nationalist community. There are some mixed areas but throughout 'the Troubles' many Catholics and Protestants have felt the need to stay in or move to communities reflecting their own cultural identity and tradition. Most young people attend schools which are only attended by Catholics or Protestants, although there are now a small number of integrated schools.

In Northern Ireland another method used in the past, and in some cases today, to keep different cultures apart has been 'endogamy'. This means only marrying individuals from the same cultural identity or religion as yourself. For example, when the Orange Order was set up, its rules stated that no member of the Order could marry or mix socially with Catholics. Similarly, the Catholic Church placed certain demands on its members if they were to marry outside the religious grouping, for example, all children born must be brought up in the Catholic faith. This process of keeping different cultures apart is referred to as '**segregation**'.

What happens when cultures live side by side?

Throughout the world many cultures have lived and continue to live side by side. However, what happens depends a great deal on whether particular groups view themselves as equal to other groups or whether they view themselves as inferior or superior. Some cultures may feel under constant threat or harassment. They may choose to deal with this by changing their lifestyle or behaviour to fit in. Alternatively they may withdraw from society and form their own smaller society within mainstream society.

Flags used as a way of marking out territory.

Painted kerbstones as a way of marking out territory.

activities

1. Using the library, Internet or Multicultural Resource Centre:
   a) list the different cultural groups who live in Northern Ireland
   b) find out the number of people who claim to belong to each cultural group.

2. Do you associate any particular symbols or signs with any of the particular groups? If yes, do any of these promote segregation?

3. Have you ever been singled out or bullied because you were considered different? How did you feel? Did you change your lifestyle or behaviour after the incident to fit in?

4. Who are the groups that are commonly singled out because of some 'difference'? Describe the reasons for these individuals or groups being singled out.

Source A

Orange march ban imposed again

Drumcree Orangemen have been banned for the sixth successive year from marching down Portadown's mainly Catholic Garvaghy Road, it was announced yesterday.

Nationalist residents welcomed the decision by the government-appointed parades commission to re-route next Sunday's annual procession. Over the past eight years, Drumcree has become Northern Ireland's most contentious marching dispute. Last year was much quieter, but even so there were 2000 police and soldiers on duty and more than 20 police officers and a handful of civilians were injured.

Yesterday the parades commission said: 'The commission has cause to believe that should the parade process the entirety of its notified route, there will be an adverse effect on community relations and a potential disorder.'

© The *Guardian*, 1 July 2003

Source B

Belfast Sectarian Violence – Injuries 16

Sixteen soldiers were injured during overnight sectarian violence in East Belfast. Troops fired 17 baton rounds in a bid to disperse gangs of rival Catholics and Protestants who were fighting along a bitterly divided peace line in the city. Security forces came under attack from stones and fireworks. Both Catholics and Protestants claim that homes had been targeted by pipe bombs on rival sides of the city divide, with property attacked on the nationalist Clandeboye Drive and the loyalist Cluan Place.

© The *Guardian*, 29 August 2003 (adapted)

activities

1. Read Sources A and B. Give reasons for the conflict that emerged in both incidents.

2. Using the Internet or local newspapers try to:

   a) gather evidence of conflict over cultural identity in the past week in Northern Ireland and record all events

   b) identify and explain conflicts over identity that exist in other countries throughout the world.

Websites you could use:
www.bbc.co.uk
www.guardian.co.uk
www.icNorthernIreland.co.uk
www.irishnews.co.uk

5. Causes and effects of stereotyping

Demonstrating in favour of women priests in 1988.

The British National Party.

While members of the same group share some common habits and values, there are numerous differences within social groups. These differences can be best described as 'sub-cultures' (smaller groups within a larger group culture which have characteristics distinct from the wider social group's culture).

Football fans undoubtedly share common characteristics, but each fan has the freedom to behave and express themselves differently from other members of the larger group of fans. For example, some fans

simply watch the match for pleasure, have friends who support other teams and are not too bothered if the team wins or loses. Other fans may be more radical. They may dislike people who support other teams, become violent and aggressive towards them if their team loses and judge people on the football team that they support. For example, violence between rival football supporters is renowned at Celtic and Rangers matches and local soccer matches. However, does this mean that all supporters of these teams are hooligans and thugs?

When we generalise about groups of people, this is called stereotyping. Look at the statements in the speech bubbles below. How are these **stereotypes**?

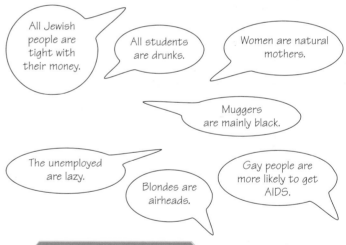

All Jewish people are tight with their money.

All students are drunks.

Women are natural mothers.

Muggers are mainly black.

The unemployed are lazy.

Blondes are airheads.

Gay people are more likely to get AIDS.

activities

1. Make a list of all the groups that you think are commonly stereotyped, for example, females, young people etc. Use the speech bubbles to help you.
2. What behaviours are associated with each group you have listed?
3. Describe what these stereotypes tell us about the way different social groups are seen and treated in our society.

5. Causes and effects of sectarianism

STAMP OUT SECTARIANISM

Give sectarianism the boot!

Sectarianism can be defined as bigoted intolerance towards other religious sects.

Religion and, in particular, the promotion of one religion at the expense of others can be a source of conflict, causing divisions and sectarianism in society. In Northern Ireland, sectarianism has become a prominent feature of many aspects of life, such as access to employment, education and housing. Housing patterns in Northern Ireland tend to be dominated by one religion or another, for example the Bogside and the Waterside in Londonderry/Derry. Similarly, in the past, the police force employed mainly Protestants. On the other hand, many Catholics were discouraged from joining the police by their own community. Sectarianism is not just found in Northern Ireland. Some other examples are given below.

◆ In the Indian sub-continent, warfare between Muslims and Hindus was partly responsible for the division of a united India into two separate countries, India and Pakistan.

◆ In the 1990s, the former country of Yugoslavia disintegrated into warring factions of Serbs, Croats and Bosnians, often aligned on religious lines.

◆ The rise of Islamic fundamentalism in the late twentieth century and early twenty-first century has seen organisations in some countries, such as the Taliban in Afghanistan, trying to remove western influences from their society.

Although differing cultural traditions can cause conflict, it would be unwise to think that aspects of cultural identity are always divisive.

activity

1. Read the following statements and try to decide whether they are examples of sectarianism.

The police favour Protestants!

Blacks out!

I don't like Catholics!

All men are the head of the household!

Prods out!

I don't like Protestants!

My religion is the best!

Fenians aren't welcome!

All Catholics are members of the IRA!

Source A

Ulster bigotry in children as young as three

The seeds of Northern Ireland's bitter sectarian hatred are taking root in children as young as 3. Pre-school youngsters were already developing **prejudices** on religion and community backgrounds. The first in-depth study of cultural and political awareness of 3–6 year olds in the region noted that some of the youngest were expressing preferences for the British or Irish flag, saying they did not like the police or Orange Order and calling those of the other religion bad. The report found that by the age of 6, 96% of children in Northern Ireland have spent at least a year at overwhelmingly segregated Catholic or Protestant primary schools, and **bigotry** was becoming worryingly ingrained in many of those surveyed, with 1 in 6 children making outright sectarian statements. For example, a 5-year-old Protestant girl said; 'The IRA and Fenians (Catholics) shoot people and wear masks' and a Catholic, aged 4 said; 'I like people who are ours. I don't like those ones because they are Orangemen. They are bad people.'

Dr Paul Connolly, University of Ulster and one of the authors of this report claimed, 'there is a notion of childhood innocence, but these children are surrounded by painted kerbstones and paramilitary murals, where daddy is going to march or granny is hanging out a flag. At the age of 3 their world view is limited, but by 5 or 6, this is turning to prejudice. They may not understand but they do absorb, and ignorance breeds sectarianism.'

© R. Cowan in the *Guardian*, 25 June 2002 (adapted)

activity

1. Read Source A. Try to identify and explain the aspects of cultural identity which appear to give rise to sectarian feelings, attitudes and behaviour.

2. Identify and explain aspects of cultural identity that create a sense of identity and nationhood for citizens of a particular country. You could consider a national flag, the history of a country, a national anthem, the language of a country, cultural organisations, etc.

The idea of '**race**' is an attempt to divide humans according to physical characteristics such as skin colour. Ethnicity is the common culture shared by a social group, such as language. An ethnic minority group is a group which shares a cultural identity, but which is different from that of the majority population of a society.

There is a wide range of ethnic groups who have emigrated to Northern Ireland and many other countries throughout the world, such as the Chinese, the Asians, the Jews and the West Indians (Afro-Caribbeans). The Irish make up a large ethnic group in Britain and America.

While many ethnic minority groups live happily alongside the cultural identity of the majority of the population, it is fair to say that some face a series of disadvantages and poorer life chances that the majority of the population don't face. These disadvantages are expressed in the form of racism, either in attitudes or behaviour.

Racism is believing or acting as though an individual or group is superior or inferior on the grounds of racial or ethnic origins, usually skin colour. This leads to those groups defined as inferior being seen as having lower intelligence and abilities. Racism involves both **racial prejudice** and **racial discrimination** and encourages hostile feelings towards groups or an individual.

The law

The Race Relations Order 1997 (Northern Ireland) made it illegal to discriminate on the grounds of race in employment and housing and to 'incite racial hatred', and Section 75 of the Northern Ireland Act 1998 strengthened this with its emphasis on **equality** of opportunity for all. However, there continues to be widespread evidence of racism and racial discrimination in employment, housing, education, the media and in many other areas. For example, in 1994 the *Sun* newspaper published the following headline after an Asian man won £18 million on the National Lottery.

VINDA LOOT!
Indian dad winner of £18 million takeaway! We're Hindi money! Happy Chap-ati!

One British Muslim, Sayyed Nadeem A. Kazmi, editor of *Islamic Dialogue*, wrote a letter to the *Guardian* newspaper claiming that these comments were evidence of racial intolerance. He argued that willingly or unwillingly the newspaper had played into the hands of those few racist elements in society. He claimed that similar comments would not have been made if it was a good 'white' family who had won. Finally he claimed that the media should be promoting racial harmony rather than giving fuel to a minority of bigots.

Source A

Ulster's shame

- People in Northern Ireland are almost twice as likely to exhibit racial prejudice as sectarian bias.
- One in four people surveyed do not want an Asian, African Caribbean or Chinese person as a neighbour.
- One in three people in Northern Ireland do not want an Asian, African Caribbean or Chinese person as a work colleague.
- Two out of three people do not want Travellers as work colleagues.
- Almost three out of every five people said they would not accept Travellers as neighbours.

© *Belfast Telegraph*, 14 April 2000 (adapted)

activities

1. In an attempt to understand cultural differences between the diverse groups in Northern Ireland, read Source A and explain how sectarianism is not the only source of conflict in Northern Ireland.

2. Research examples of racism. You could contact the Equality Commission for Northern Ireland. Report back on what racial prejudice and discrimination individuals or groups may have faced.

Racism – fact or fiction?

A government report published in 2002 claimed that in broad terms ethnic minority groups such as Black Caribbeans, Pakistanis and Bangladeshis are disadvantaged in the labour market (*Ethnic Minorities and the Labour Market*, Cabinet Office, 2002). For example, in 2001/2, unemployment rates by ethnic groups were as follows:

- Whites 4.7%
- Black African 14.1%
- Indian 7.3%
- Pakistani 16.1%
- Black Caribbean 11.6%
- Bangladeshi 21.3%

Inequalities in the labour market.

Racial attacks

Black and Asian people are the victims of more crimes of violence than white people. The British Crime Survey found that there were 280,000 racially motivated offences in Britain in 1999. An example of a racially motivated murder in Northern Ireland is the case of Simon Tang. He was beaten with clubs outside his family's Chinese restaurant in 1996 and died from his injuries a short time later. James Hawthorne from the Commission for Racial Equality said that there were racial undertones in his murder. The police at the time stated that 'the trouble with these people is they tend not to use banks'. This would appear to highlight institutional racism in the police force, but James Hawthorne argues that racism is more than just a police problem – it's a community problem.

Is it fair to say that in Northern Ireland we focus so much on the 'two main communities' that we forget there are other communities and groups? There are 8000 Chinese in Northern Ireland and they are the single biggest ethnic minority here. Throughout the past few years there has been a rapidly growing ethnic minority population. For example, in Dungannon there have been increasing numbers of Portuguese working in factories and hospitals and there are growing numbers of specialists being employed from India and the Philippines.

Is racism still a problem?

The British and Northern Ireland governments are trying to get rid of racism within major institutions. They have removed recruitment, selection and promotion procedures which might discriminate against ethnic groups. They have introduced race awareness courses, monitoring of job applications and equal opportunities policies to prevent racism at work. Despite these measures, problems related to racism continue. The first black police chief constable was only appointed in the UK in 2003. Statistics show that people in Northern Ireland are more likely to marry someone from the opposite religion than from a different race. Does this mean racism is a bigger problem than sectarianism? How many local **councillors** are non-white? How many of our local politicians are non-white?

8. The development of human rights

As previously discussed, cultural diversity can pose many challenges for a society. The negative results of this are stereotyping, racism and sectarianism. The key question is how do governments, institutions and individuals prevent cultural diversity continuing to be a source of conflict and encourage it to be viewed and accepted as a source of enrichment? For example:

- How do we stop racism?
- How do we reduce sectarian tensions?
- How as a society can we prevent discrimination on the basis of race, religion, etc.?

These issues and questions have formed the basis of many human rights declarations and conventions in contemporary societies such as Britain and Northern Ireland.

The origins of human rights

Ideas and notions of human rights are not something new and are not confined to countries such as Britain and Northern Ireland. Many of us think that rights are something that all human beings should be able to expect no matter what, but people haven't always had rights. We only have rights when laws are passed and agreements made between governments about them. The concept of people having human rights has developed over centuries. Many events have helped lead to the setting up of accepted human rights in different parts of the world.

The idea of 'rights' began to emerge as long ago as 1215 with the Magna Carta. In that year King John of England was forced into signing a document called the Magna Carta which provided barons (rich landowners) with rights such as the following:

- tax could not be forced on the barons without their consent
- laws could only be passed with the consent of bishops, earls and barons.

Even though this document only promised rights for the barons, many regarded it as the first set of human rights written into the law in Britain. This tradition was then followed by the American Declaration of Independence in 1776 and the Declaration of the Rights of Man in France in 1789.

In the aftermath of the Second World War, many countries believed there was an urgent need for an agreement that would set out human rights for people all over the world, not just the people of individual countries. In 1948 the Universal Declaration of Human Rights (UDHR) was adopted. The countries that signed the declaration made a commitment to their citizens and to each other that they would strive to protect these 'human rights'. Nearly every country in the world has now signed the declaration, which has 30 articles.

activities

1. Rewrite each human right from the table opposite in your own words, explaining what it means to you.

2. Identify and explain one example of how each right may have been denied to individuals or groups in your community or other communities throughout the world.

The Universal Declaration of Human Rights

Everyone . . .

1. Is born free and should be treated in the same way	16. Has the right to marry
2. Is equal despite differences in colour, **sex**, language, etc.	17. Has the right to own property and things
3. Has the right to life and to live in freedom and safety	18. Has the right to freedom of thought, conscience and religion
4. Should be free from slavery	19. Has the right to freedom of opinion and expression
5. Has the right not to be hurt or tortured	20. Has the right to meet with others
6. Has the right to be recognised before the law	21. Has the right to take part in government and vote
7. Has the right to be treated equally before the law	22. Has the right to social security
8. Has the right to ask for legal help when their rights are not respected	23. Has the right to work and join a trade union
9. Has the right not to be imprisoned unjustly	24. Has the right to rest and leisure
10. Has the right to a fair trial	25. Has the right to an adequate standard of living and medical help
11. Has the right to be presumed innocent until proven guilty	26. Has the right to go to school
12. Has the right to privacy	27. Has the right to take part in their community's cultural life
13. Has the right to travel within and to and from their own country	28. Is entitled to a social and international order that is necessary for these rights
14. Has the right to asylum	29. Must respect the rights of others
15. Has the right to a nationality	30. Finally, no one can take away any of the rights in this declaration

9. International human rights

International abuses of human rights are extensive – probably worse than you have ever imagined. The information on this page comes mainly from Amnesty International and other charities.

USA
In the past 20 years, it has been proved that over 75 death row inmates were wrongly convicted. The death penalty is most commonly used on blacks. Juvenile offenders and mentally impaired individuals have also been executed. **Asylum seekers** are sometimes treated as criminals.

UK
Forty people under 18 commit suicide in British prisons every year. Under children's rights they should not be there.

Jamaica
Since the formation of a 'Crime Management Unit' (CMU) in 2000, there have been numerous allegations of human rights violations and **extra-judicial executions**. In 2002 the police killed 133 people yet rarely face prosecution.

Pakistan
Infamous for its **blasphemy laws**, since 11 September there have been increasing attacks on Christian properties and people, including a Christmas Day grenade attack which killed three girls.

Iraq
Mass graves of executed Iraqis have been found. Amnesty has recorded 17,000 disappearances.

Honduras
Extra-judicial executions of 15,000 street children by state agents or unidentified individuals have been reported.

Turkey
BP oil pipeline construction threatens land and water for 30,000 people. Protesters are at serious risk of rights abuses. British taxpayers' money funds the project.

Algeria
After a long civil war Algeria has not investigated the 'disappearances' of thousands of civilians by security forces.

Colombia
The civil war has seen widespread human rights violations by security forces and armed groups, including the assassinations of 184 trade unionists, 17,000 abductions and arbitrary detentions, disappearances and exiles. Ten families per hour flee their homes; 28,000 people are killed annually.

Paraguay
Children under 18 (sometimes as young as 12) are illegally and possibly forcibly recruited into the police and army. Ill treatment occurs often and some conscripts under 18 have died in unclear circumstances.

Sudan

A 20-year civil war fuelled by oil and religious extremism has cost 2 million lives and created a million refugees. Serious human rights abuses including torture, rape and arbitrary killings are widely reported.

Children's rights?

- 11 million children under 5 die annually from preventable diseases.
- By 2010 in 12 African countries 15% of children will be orphans due to AIDS and war.
- 12 million children lost their homes in natural disasters and wars in the last 10 years.
- Six million children have been killed or maimed in conflict in the last 10 years.
- 110 million children of primary school age have no education. Two-thirds are girls.

Development

- If you have never experienced the danger of battle, imprisonment, torture or starvation, you are ahead of 500 million people in the world.
- If you have food in your fridge, clothes on your back and a roof over your head then you are richer than 75% of the world's population.
- 50% suffer from malnutrition.
- 1.2 billion people live on less than 70p per day.

Russia

In a state with increasing extremism, racism and censorship, journalists and environmentalists labelled 'dangerous' have been jailed. Harsh conditions, torture, executions and ill treatment are reported.

Lebanon

Prisoners have been reportedly tortured to force 'confessions'. American pressure after 11 September led to arbitrary arrests of Muslims.

India/Bangladesh border

Tensions over border migration have led to mass expulsions, nationality disputes and arbitrary arrests. Stranded people are kept in 'no man's land' without adequate shelter or facilities.

Philippines

Up to 20,000 street children are prisoners. Held in adult jails without charge, trial or explanation, they are abused by adults. Eight young people on death row were under age at the time of their offence.

activity

Which of these human rights abuses shocks you most and why?

Amnesty International information:

- 63 countries hold **prisoners of conscience**.
- 72 countries have imprisoned people without charge.
- 125 countries torture prisoners.
- Extra-judicial executions have apparently happened in 61 countries.
- 1457 prisoners were executed in 28 countries in the year 2000.
- 'Disappearances' have happened in 30 countries.

Nigeria

Regular religious rioting occurs against non-Muslims. In riots in November 2002, 500 died, 1200 were injured and 12,000 became homeless.

Zimbabwe

Under strict Muslim (Sharia) laws, unmarried women with children can face death by stoning for adultery. Laws silencing criticism and objection were made.

10. International human rights laws

Covenants

It is important to remember that almost every country in the world signed the UDHR (see pages 20–21). This demonstrates the promise or commitment of each country's government to the principles of promoting and protecting human rights. However, it is not a legally binding document. A declaration is a statement of hope or opinion. This means that countries have not necessarily translated these rights into laws which are legally binding. In 1966, two covenants were introduced which attempted to make the principles of the UDHR legally binding and have become known as the international '**Bill of Rights**' (see page 44).

1. International Covenant on Civil and Political Rights (1966)
2. International Covenant on Economic, Social and Cultural Rights (1966)

In the following decades, specialised legal texts were developed to make sure that rights laid down in the UDHR and the two International Covenants above would apply directly to particular groups within society, for example:

◆ Convention on Asylum (1951)
◆ Convention on the Elimination of Racial Discrimination (1969)
◆ Convention against Torture (1984)
◆ Convention on the Rights of the Child (1989).

These treaties and many others make up international human rights law, which holds states (governments) accountable for their actions towards their citizens. These treaties are attempts to legislate against types of behaviour and language which may promote exclusion of groups or individuals rather than their inclusion into society as equals. The UN (United Nations) and national governments have the responsibility of making sure that countries who signed the treaties keep to the principles laid down in each.

The ECHR

The **European Convention on Human Rights** (ECHR) was introduced in 1953. Its principles were inspired by the UDHR and the countries and their governments who signed the treaty have a legal obligation to make sure that their citizens enjoy the rights that are laid down within the treaty. The European Court of Human Rights at Strasbourg is the 'judicial organ' (the court which ensures that all rights laid down in the ECHR are upheld). This means that if individuals or groups feel that their rights have been violated, they can take their case to this court. If the European Court finds that the rights of the individual or group have been violated, then the government of that country will be called upon to change its laws in order to comply with the ECHR. On 2 October 2000, the ECHR became part of **domestic law** in the UK. It was called the **Human Rights Act**.

To practise faith.

To vote.

Freedom of speech.

These are some of the rights enshrined in the Human Rights Act.

The UNCRC

The United Nations Convention on the Rights of the Child (UNCRC) is a promise made by the government to young people under the age of 18 years. When the UK government signed it in 1991, they agreed that children and young people are citizens who have a number of rights and they agreed to make sure this promise is kept. The government works through several bodies on a daily basis, including the Department of Education (DENI), the Police Service of Northern Ireland (PSNI) and Health and Social Services. Each of these bodies helps the government to keep its promise. The UNCRC has been signed by almost half the countries in the world. Below is a brief summary of the rights of the child.

◆ Children have a right to be with their family or those who will care for them best.

◆ Children have the right to an adequate standard of living.

◆ Children have the right to health care.

◆ Disabled children have a right to special care and training.

◆ Children must be allowed to speak their own language and practise their own culture and religion.

◆ Children have a right to play.

◆ Children have the right to free education.

◆ Children have the right to be kept safe and not hurt, exploited or neglected.

◆ Children must not be used as cheap labour or soldiers.

◆ Children have the right to protection from cruelty, neglect and injustice.

◆ Children have the right to express their own opinions and to meet together to express their views.

activities

1. For each of the rights listed opposite, try to describe a real event from your local area or from further away when these rights have been denied.

2. Identify which rights from the UNCRC the following cases could be considered to have violated.
   - A school bus is targeted with stones and missiles; five children had to receive hospital treatment.
   - An 8-year-old 'Traveller' is refused a place at a local school.
   - A child is smacked for misbehaving.
   - A student is expelled from school and cannot sit GCSEs in any other school.
   - A 6-year-old girl is spat at in a local park and told to go back to where she came from.
   - A school refuses to allow female Muslims to attend classes in traditional dress.
   - Disabled children can't gain access to a local swimming pool.
   - A 3-year-old child is found home alone as its parents go on a drinking binge.
   - A 4-year-old child works 60 hours a week.
   - Two toddlers escape injury after they were targeted because of their football shirts.

11. Bill of Rights for Northern Ireland

Most countries throughout the world have a variety of diverse groups. In Northern Ireland, the consequences of racism, sectarianism and stereotyping different cultural groups has led to some groups being segregated from others. The government wants to ensure that diversity and inclusion can exist side by side in Northern Irish society and this has led to calls for a Bill of Rights.

Bill of Rights

For many years and in particular since the Belfast (Good Friday) Agreement there have been calls for a Bill of Rights in Northern Ireland. Consequently, after the Agreement was signed the Northern Ireland Human Rights Commission began to consult with all members and groups in Northern Ireland to ensure a Bill of Rights for Northern Ireland. As yet, however, it has not become a reality. When completed, this Bill of Rights will include specific rights related to the country's situation and will include the human rights laid done in the ECHR.

Under the Belfast (Good Friday) Agreement it states that the Bill of Rights should 'Reflect the particular circumstances of Northern Ireland' and that 'These additional rights [are] to reflect the principles of mutual respect for the identity and ethos of both communities and parity of esteem'. These rights could include social, economic, civil, cultural and political rights (see page 47 for more information about the Bill of Rights).

What should be in the Bill of Rights for Northern Ireland?

The Universal Declaration of Human Rights (1948) sets out the basic rights of all people.
Here are just a few of the Rights enshrined in the document:
Everyone
• *Is born free and should be treated in the same way.*
• *Is equal despite differences in colour, sex, language etc.*
• *Should be free from slavery.*
• *Has the right not to be imprisoned unjustly.*
• *Has the right to work.*
• *Has the right to go to school.*

A new Bill of Rights is being planned for Northern Ireland. What Rights do you think should be included in the document?

Everyone will have the Right...

activities

1. Debate the following issues.
   • Is a Bill of Rights necessary for Northern Ireland or could the UK Human Rights Act be applied to Northern Ireland?
   • Should the Bill only include the rights of the two main traditions?
   • Should the Bill include a special chapter on children's rights or should there be a separate Bill of Rights for children?
   • Should Northern Ireland set up a special Human Rights Court?

2. If you were creating a Bill of Rights for Northern Ireland, what rights would you include relating to: Women, Children, Victims, Education, Environment, Languages, Equality?

3. Take a copy of the proposed Bill of Rights and submit a response either as a group or as an individual to the Northern Ireland Human Rights Commission outlining what you feel should be included in it. (A copy of the proposed Bill can be obtained from the NIHRC, Belfast.)

Does Northern Ireland need a Bill of Rights?

Section 75 of the Northern Ireland Act ensured equality laws and rights.

Promoting inclusion?

Clearly it is hoped that a Bill of Rights for Northern Ireland will emerge in the future. However, it is also important that individuals and groups promote inclusion of everyone in our society to ensure that each of us can enjoy our human rights. One way to ensure that Northern Ireland is a **civil society** is to strive to recognise and celebrate differences between all groups and allow these to develop into constructive relationships with each other.

Perhaps the most difficult response to the extent of cultural diversity in any society is to respect the beliefs, rights and traditions of all social groups. Respecting other social groups is no easy task but it does not mean that we should assume that 'our' group is superior to 'their' group.

Final thought

'... Those from either side of the divide who can't leave their hatred and bitterness behind cannot be allowed to blight the lives of others ...'

John Reid (Former Secretary of State for Northern Ireland), 3 October 2001

activities

1. Below are some quotes from a variety of ethnic groups saying how they have experienced life in Northern Ireland. Read the quotes and try to explain whether diversity is always a source of conflict.

> I enjoy living in Northern Ireland. The people here are so friendly and they will go out of their way to help you. I also love Northern Ireland's countryside. It is so beautiful.
>
> *Mrs A.S. Khan, Belfast Islamic Centre*

> I came to Northern Ireland in 1993. I have no problems living here so far.
>
> *Mrs A. Graham, N.I. Filipino Association*

> As an ethnic minority, it is difficult to adjust to our culture. If I had a choice I would bring my children up in the Sudanese way of life.
>
> *Ameer Ibrahim, Ballymena*

> People look at ethnic minorities as immigrants. They do not appreciate that people were born here. This is their home!
>
> *Dr Mamoun Mobayed, Belfast Islamic Centre (NICEM – Northern Ireland Council for Ethnic Minorities)*

2. Is there anything that we as individuals can do to help promote inclusion? Try to make a list of what we can do.
3. Describe whether you believe that cultural diversity enriches a community or poses challenges for it.

introduction

The second section of this textbook is about 'Equality and Social Justice'. It follows on from the previous section, which ended with a consideration of strategies for promoting inclusion of everyone within society. It explores how inequalities can arise in two main ways. For example, some may face discrimination and inequality because of their group identity (gender, disability, ethnic group, etc.). Others may experience inequality on the basis of their material circumstances (for example, homeless people, asylum seekers, unemployed people). In particular, it examines how **discrimination** can occur at an individual and institutional level (organisations, places of work). Finally, it should help you to develop an understanding of how governments and voluntary organisations can promote equality and social justice and the role of **human rights standards**.

12. What is equality and social justice?

Equality

Equality means that everybody has the same rights to dignity, respect, protection and opportunity. Each society needs to safeguard the individual and **collective rights** of its people to ensure that everyone is treated equally and fairly. This means that no individual or group should feel or be excluded (left out) from any aspect of social life. Everyone must have the same opportunities and access to education, to work, to housing, to leisure facilities, to practise their faith, etc.

Social justice

Justice refers to the right of each person to be treated fairly. Social justice refers to the idea that everybody in society should be treated fairly. However, treating everyone fairly does not mean treating everyone equally. For example, vulnerable people such as the homeless may need more help than those who are not homeless. Some examples of social justice issues are given below.

- Unemployment – Northern Ireland has one of the highest rates of unemployment in the UK (5.6%), coming close behind Scotland at 5.8%. Unemployment in Wales stands at 4.7% (September 2003 Labour Market Trends).

- Poverty – This causes great injustices for many groups throughout the world. For example, UNICEF (the United Nations Children's Fund) claim that 1.2 billion people in the world are living on a dollar (about 60p) a day. They have estimated

that half of these are children – representing 40% of all children under 18 in developing countries (United Nations Development Programme 2000). In Great Britain in 2000, 25% of the population, some 14 million people, were living on half the average weekly income.

What are the consequences of these injustices? How can individuals, groups and governments work to ensure equality and social justice for everyone? If we take the issues above, it is clear that individuals who suffer from unemployment and poverty are excluded from participating in many parts of society and do not have access to all society's products and services.

The Welfare State

In the past, the British government tried to develop strategies to ensure that individuals who suffered from these disadvantages were not excluded from participating in society. For example, in 1948 the Welfare State was introduced in England, Scotland, Wales and Northern Ireland. This involved the creation of the National Health Service (NHS), free schools and social security systems. Many felt that this would eradicate the social injustices that were the products of poverty and unemployment. However, each year around 800,000 families fail to claim benefits they are entitled to. According to the Department for Work and Pensions, an estimated £2 billion of benefits was unclaimed in 1999–2000.

Children sifting through rubbish for food in Calcutta, India.

Many researchers into this area maintain that this is due to the complexity of the benefit system, the obscure language of the leaflets and the inadequate publicity, which means that individuals and groups often do not know their rights or the procedures for claiming benefits. Thus, they continue to be socially disadvantaged.

activities

1. Look at the two speech bubbles. Is there any evidence of **inequality**? Are these social justice issues?

2. Describe the inequalities that each individual to the right has highlighted.

3. What do you think is meant by equality? Is equality the same as everybody being treated the same? Give reasons for your answer.

4. Are there some individuals or groups who should be treated differently to ensure they are being treated equally? Give reasons for your answer.

5. Discuss a time when you felt you were treated unfairly or you witnessed someone being treated unfairly.

Slum housing in Rio de Janeiro, Brazil.

What is equality?

I live in Belfast. It is a very friendly place.

But sometimes people make me feel different.

Sometimes when we have discussions they say, 'What do you think?'

Why do they necessarily think I will have a different opinion?

Is it because I'm Hindu?

I get up each morning at seven.

I make breakfast and school lunches.

I take the kids to school then I go home, clean the kitchen, make the beds and put on a wash.

I pick up the kids from school, help them with homework and make the dinner.

Then when my husband comes home, he asks, 'What happened in the living room? Have you been watching TV all day?'

Equality and Social Justice

13. How do inequalities arise?

Inequalities between people in any society can arise as a result of differences such as gender, disability, sexuality and ethnic group.

Many of us may be uncomfortable about differences between people. Even very young children may have formed attitudes towards different groups or individuals and can **scapegoat** (blame/discriminate) somebody on the basis of some physical or other difference. For example, children as young as 3 have made comments such as, 'I like people who are ours' (see page 17). Discrimination on the basis of these differences leads to inequalities in society. People are often discriminated against because of their:

- gender
- disability
- race
- sexuality.

1. Gender inequalities

Girl power!

Although during the twentieth and twenty-first centuries the status of women has gradually improved, with women now having job opportunities and rights that were previously denied them, it would appear that women are still not treated as equals with men in the workplace. There continues to be a 'sexual division of labour' where jobs are divided into 'men's jobs' and 'women's jobs'. For example, after the 2001 General Election, only 18% of British MPs and 3% of senior police officers (superintendent and above) were women.

Many feminists would argue that the jobs that women do are extensions of their traditional domestic roles as housewives and mothers, for example, nursing, teaching, secretarial work and low-grade jobs such as waitresses and cleaners. Women make up two-thirds of people working in public administration, education and health. Also, women are more likely to work part-time. In 2000, out of the 6.9 million part-time workers in the UK, 5.5 million were women. Women continue to be paid less than men. For example, in 2003 a report from the Equality Commission Northern Ireland claimed that women are still being paid 19% less than men in equivalent jobs.

activity

Carry out a small survey to find out the kind of jobs men and women in your local area do. You could ask members of your family or neighbours in your street.

2. Disability

Disability rights groups demonstrate for equal rights.

Katrina's Story

I didn't always use a wheelchair. I didn't like using it in front of other kids because it always made me feel different. So my mum got me some patches and kneepads so I could crawl about in the street with the other kids. I must have gone through a pair of jeans a week! The neighbours would all go on at her saying, 'what are you doing, letting her go about like that?' But she didn't care, she wasn't going to wrap me up in cotton wool or make me stay in the house. She took me for what I was – always.

One morning I woke up when I was 16, I hated my disability. I never really noticed the way I was before, or I hadn't made a big deal of it. But then I woke up and realised I was different. And I hated it. I wouldn't go anywhere or speak to anyone on the phone. I was very depressed. I was at a special school and had been getting good grades. But, when I went through this bad patch, I stopped working. What was the point in working? Whether you got an A or a U the teachers treated you as if you were great anyway, simply because you were disabled. When my brother got a U my mother went haywire but when I got a U it didn't matter. So I just gave up. The teachers took the view that if they prepared us for the outside world that was enough. And even then the teachers didn't have a clue. And as for sex education … you must be joking! We were disabled people – we weren't supposed to be interested in that!

Adapted from the *Belfast Telegraph*, 8 April 2001

3. Racism

Newsflash 15 October 2003

A lone mother and her two young children living in County Armagh became the latest victims of a violent racist campaign. The family who are believed to be Muslim are the latest victims of attacks on the Muslim community living in the area. The family home came under attack around 11:30 pm where a number of windows were smashed. This attack backdrops a leafleting campaign in the area by a **white supremacy** racist group attacking the proposal for a permanent mosque to be built in the area.

activity

Discuss the opportunities that some ethnic groups are denied, such as the right to a home.

4. Sexuality

The human rights of sexual minorities are systematically abused in much of the world today. Around 2% of the world's female population and 4% of the world's male population live exclusively as homosexuals. Laws against them tend to focus on homosexual practice, but they may also affect **transgender** people. Progressive equality and anti-discrimination **legislation** is getting onto the statute books in some countries throughout the world.

Given below are some facts about equalities and inequalities relating to sexuality.

- Legal recognition of same sex relationships exists in Denmark, France, Iceland, Hungary, Sweden, Netherlands, Norway, Greenland, Quebec (Canada) and Vermont (US).
- Iran, Afghanistan and Saudi Arabia are known to have executed homosexuals for their sexuality during the past decade.
- Violent attacks on or harassment of sexual minorities and AIDS activists have been reported in 19 countries since 1994.
- Severe police harassment of sexual minorities has been reported in 18 countries.
- Gays and lesbians are banned from the armed forces in Japan, Belarus, Croatia, Greece, Hungary, Luxembourg, Poland, Portugal, Turkey, Argentina, Peru, Brazil and Venezuela.

activity

Find out if the law in Northern Ireland promotes equality on the basis of sexuality. You could contact your MP or look at the Northern Ireland Assembly's website.

14. Protecting equality

How can we as individuals, as a society and as a government respond to inequalities?

The role of the government

The government of a democratic country and its justice system has the responsibility to protect the rights of individuals and groups. It should ensure that each individual has the right to dignity, respect, protection and opportunity. The law of a country should be constructed in such a way as to ensure that no individual or group experiences discrimination or inequalities. The government can communicate to its citizens the desire for equality and social justice through various forms of the media and can educate its citizens in schools and community groups.

So what role does the law in Northern Ireland play in protecting each of its citizens from inequalities and social injustices?

The main pieces of equality legislation in Northern Ireland are:

◆ **Equal Pay Act (Northern Ireland) 1970 (amended 1984)**
This act applies equally to men and women of all ages and its purpose is to eliminate discrimination between the sexes in pay and in other terms of their contracts of employment such as holidays and sick leave.

◆ **Sex Discrimination (Northern Ireland) Order 1976 (amended 1988)**
This order makes it unlawful to discriminate against an individual on the basis of his or her sex in the fields of employment, training and related matters, education, the provision of goods, facilities and services and the disposal and management of premises.

◆ **Race Relations (Northern Ireland) Order 1997**
This order outlaws discrimination on the basis of colour, race, nationality or ethnic or national origin.

◆ **Fair Employment and Treatment (Northern Ireland) Order 1998**
This order makes it unlawful to discriminate against someone on the basis of religious belief or political opinion. This includes a person's supposed religious or political opinion and the absence of any, or any particular belief or political opinion.

◆ **Disability Discrimination Act 1995**
This act introduced new rights for disabled people in areas of employment and access to goods, facilities, services and premises. It introduced a duty for businesses to make reasonable adjustments to help overcome the practical effects of a disability.

◆ **Northern Ireland Act 1998**
After the Belfast (Good Friday) Agreement which was signed by both the British and Irish governments and almost all the political parties in Northern Ireland, a new law called the Northern Ireland Act 1998 was passed. This law set up a local assembly and gave our politicians the power to make decisions about most things in Northern Ireland. Part of this law was about 'equality'. This part is called Section 75 (S75). S75 requires public authorities (government bodies like the Department of Education, Health & Social Services, Education and Library Boards, Housing Executive etc.) to have due regard to the need to promote equality of opportunity between certain groups, such as between men and women, between persons with or without a disability, between persons of different religious belief, political opinion, racial group, age, marital status or sexual orientation, and between persons with or without dependants.

The British and Northern Ireland governments are committed to protecting the individual and group rights of all their citizens to ensure that everyone is treated fairly and justly. However, it is worthwhile mentioning that each of us as individuals and as groups also have a role to play in the promotion of equality, justice and freedom to ensure that our country is a fairer place to live in for all citizens.

activity

Read the following cases below and:

a) describe the inequalities that each individual or group may have faced

b) decide which legislation relates to each case.

Five members of the Travelling community refused permission to play on local golf course

Discounted family swim passes, two adults and two children £10

Females continue to be paid 19% less than their male counterparts

Woman sacked for being pregnant

Muslim family's home attacked at the weekend

Two men and a woman who described themselves as vampires were found guilty of religiously aggravated harassment against a vicar and his family

Local council refused Catholic man promotion when they voted for candidates along party lines

The role of the individual

'We are the hero of our own story'
M.T. McCarthy US 1912-1989 (US writer, critie and educator)

It is true that one person cannot change the world, but that is no reason to give up and say, 'I can't change anything, I'm only one person.' If individuals in the past had taken that position, many advances may not have taken place in Northern Ireland. For example, George Mitchell, the US Peace Envoy under President Clinton, did not give up with the peace process. He worked tirelessly with all the political parties in Northern Ireland until the Belfast (Good Friday) Agreement was signed and voted for by the citizens of Northern Ireland.

It is important to point out that many individuals make a difference every day. For example, many make donations to organisations such as Age Concern and The Simon Community. Some write letters to their local councillors and MPs to highlight their concerns and ask for government support on particular issues. Others may protest in their opposition to what they see as inequalities. For example, some students see top-up fees for university as unjust so they protest about this perceived inequality. Others volunteer their help and time to organisations such as Gingerbread (which helps to support single parents). These individuals are trying in their own way (small or large) to promote equality of opportunity for each individual and group who lives in Northern Ireland. So maybe the motto should be, 'Ask not what your country can do for you but what you can do for your country' (from John F. Kennedy's inaugural speech in 1960).

The role of society

'United we stand, divided we fall.' The idea behind this statement is that if we form groups to promote equality and social justice, we have a better chance of succeeding. When groups of individuals come together to promote equality and social justice, they have immense power to affect the country in which they live. Numerous and varied **NGOs (non-governmental organisations)** exist in Northern Ireland. The primary and central focus of each NGO is to promote a culture of equality and social justice.

15. Social justice matters

Social justice refers to opportunities to ensure that social issues and problems such as unemployment, poverty and homelessness do not blight our society and the lives of its citizens. Unlike equality, it focuses on particular issues rather than individuals or groups. This section explores three examples of such issues in Northern Ireland.

1. Poverty

Speech bubble: Poverty? What poverty?

Label: HOMELESS

Has poverty gone?

◆ In 2001, the poorest 50% of the British population owned only 5% of the wealth in the UK, while the richest 1% owned approximately 25% of the wealth in the UK (Inland Revenue 2001).

◆ The picture appears even bleaker when we examine the unequal distribution of income in the UK. The richest fifth of income earners saw an income growth of 9% from 1978 to 2000, whereas the poorest fifth of income earners saw an income decrease of 0.4% over the same period (Department of Social Security 1999/2000).

◆ Of those living in poverty, 12% were unemployed, 38% were self-employed or were in full-time or part-time work in low-paid jobs, 19% were pensioners and 21% were single parents (Department of Social Security 2001).

activities

1. Do you think poverty really exists in Britain and Northern Ireland, given the starving population in Ethiopia, for example?

2. Either individually or as part of a group try to draw up a list of necessities that you believe every individual should be able to afford and no one should have to go without.

3. Imagine that you have become First Minister for Northern Ireland. You have a huge majority supporting you in government and will be able to start a successful attack against poverty. Try to construct a series of policies that you believe will combat poverty in Northern Ireland. For each policy explain how it would eliminate poverty.

2. Homelessness

Homelessness is a real and ever-increasing problem in Northern Ireland. In 2000/01 the Housing Executive recorded 14,000 people as homeless. This means that around 1 in every 73 people in Northern Ireland were homeless in 2000/01. Over half the people who approached the Simon Community last year were aged 17–25. Around a quarter were aged 16–18 and around a quarter were female. Each year the Simon Community receives around 4000 requests for assistance from those who are homeless. However, due to financial constraints it can only help around 1000 people. This means that for every four people who come, they can only help one.

1. Research investigation: The Simon Community. Find out the answers to the following questions and include them in a short report on the organisation. (The Simon Community's website is www.simoncommunity.org.uk)

   • What does the Simon Community do?

   • Who is Simon?

   • In what year did the Simon Community open in Northern Ireland?

   • How many people work for the Simon Community?

   • What are the causes of homelessness?

   • What is the age range of homeless people?

   • What happens to those who cannot be helped by the Simon Community?

   • Why are there so many people homeless in Northern Ireland when there are so many empty flats?

2. Organise a class or school debate on the issue of homelessness in Northern Ireland. The motion for the debate is 'The right to adequate housing should be included in the Bill of Rights for Northern Ireland'. You will need:

   • a chairperson

   • five speakers for the opposition

   • five speakers for the proposition

   • participants from the audience to question the opposition and proposition.

3. Ageing population

It's the flu epidemic again. We'll have to add another six months to the waiting list.

Some of the consequences of an ageing population.

According to the 2001 census for Northern Ireland, some 16% of the population are of pensionable age. In the UK, 1.1 million people are over the age of 85 and around 22% of the population are over the age of 60 (UK 2001 Census). Some would argue that the growing proportion of elderly people in the population has created a growing burden of dependence. This suggests that the elderly are viewed as a problem. For example, some have suggested that the ageing population has led to:

◆ increases in taxes to pay the costs of benefits for the elderly

◆ rising youth unemployment

◆ housing shortages

◆ longer waiting lists in the NHS.

It is imperative to remember that each of us will grow old. Will we have to face similar injustices at an individual and institutional level?

1. Identify and explain two problems for the individual facing old age in society today.

2. Explain fully two problems for society of an ageing population.

3. Interview an elderly relative or neighbour and ask them to explain the advantages and problems they face as they get older.

35

16. Promoting social justice

Promoting social justice around the globe. We all have a part to play.

How can we as individuals, as a society and as a government respond to social justices that affect our country?

As can be seen, social injustices occur at an individual and institutional level, thus individuals, societies and governments all have a part to play. However, one must note that there are difficulties in trying to promote social justice as resources are often limited.

The role of the individual

As an individual, we may consider that social justice issues will never affect us. But in reality, social injustices can affect every one of us. For example, are you sure you will get a job when you leave school? Will you always have a home? Will you never grow old? These are real issues for many people in Northern Irish society, which don't always carry easy answers or solutions. As an individual, you can make a difference to promote social justice in Northern Ireland. For example, you can help by:

◆ donating to those NGOs whose aim is to promote social justice for disadvantaged groups

◆ campaigning

◆ raising awareness in your school and community

◆ volunteering your help to NGOs or charities in your community or school

◆ writing a proposal of what you think should be in the Bill of Rights for Northern Ireland and sending it to the NIHRC.

All of the above activities can make a difference to the local community and to Northern Ireland as a whole.

The role of society

A vast array of NGOs exists in Northern Ireland to try to combat social injustices such as poverty, unemployment and homelessness. Each organisation's central aim is to promote a culture of rights, equality and social justice for each citizen living in Northern Ireland. For example, Age Concern Northern Ireland's role has been to ensure that the views and needs of an ageing population are considered in government policy. The organisation would claim that those who maintain that the elderly are a burden and that we can't afford to subsidise their living are wrong. They would strongly contend that as a society 'we can't afford not to, surely the elderly should have an equal share in the wealth that they have undoubtedly played a role in creating' (Dr J. McKenna, Chairperson, Age Concern Northern Ireland).

The role of the government

Current legislation on equality and social justice (see page 32) shows that, theoretically at least, the governments of Northern Ireland and Britain are committed to the promotion and protection of equality and social justice for all their citizens. However, it is important that individuals know their rights and that those governments ensure that individuals and institutions uphold the equality agenda. In Northern Ireland we have the Equality Commission, which aims to promote respect for diversity, eliminate discrimination and achieve equality of opportunity for all. It has a duty to keep equality and social justice legislation under review and to advise the government on recommendations for change.

17. How fair is our world?

We tend to be generally aware, through watching TV or hearing from charities or NGOs, that things are not very equal across our world. What are the causes and consequences of these inequalities and social injustices and exactly how 'unfair' is our planet?

What forms can global inequalities take?

Teenage issues?
'The real issues for youth in Africa are not different from the issues of young people everywhere. Will I find a job? Will I find the love of my life? Will I be safe and secure? The great difference is that in Africa, a young person has a 4% chance of finding work after finishing school, at least a 10% chance of being infected by HIV by the love of his or her life, and probably a 50% chance of being a victim or perpetrator of crime or violent attack. Not very nice odds, when you are a 16 year old, on the brink of adulthood.'

Young Africa by Reinhild Niebuhr

If the population of the world was just 100 people:
'57 would be Asians, 21 Europeans, 14 from the Americas and eight Africans. Six would have 59% of the world's wealth, 80 would live in sub-standard housing, 70 would be illiterate, 50 would suffer from malnutrition, one would have higher education and one would own a computer.'

Just Right (Jubilee Action Magazine)

Telly addicts?
'24% of British children aged under 4 have a TV set in their bedrooms.'

Daily Telegraph, 2000

Fair trade coffee?
'For every latte sold in Starbucks at £1.95 a throw, the farmer in Guatemala will receive 2p.'

Guardian/Action Aid, 2000

37

Cow power!
Every year, livestock in rich countries get more money than poor people in the developing world.

EU subsidy per cow: $803	Ethiopia income per person: $100
USA subsidy per cow: $1057	Bangladesh income per person: $360
Japan subsidy per cow: $2555	Honduras income per person: $920

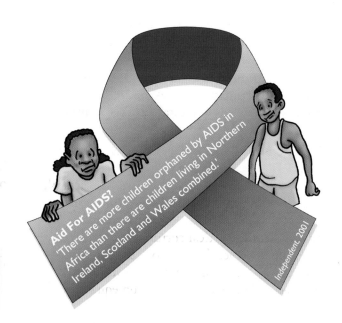

Aid For AIDS?
'There are more children orphaned by AIDS in Africa than there are children living in Northern Ireland, Scotland and Wales combined.'

Independent, 2001

The Great Divide
High income countries have 16% of the world population and 80% of the world GDP (Gross Domestic Product). Low income countries have 40% of the world population and 3% of the world GDP.

Tariffs
A developing country could earn more money for its goods if it processed them. However, the EU places low tariffs on tomatoes, higher ones on tinned tomatoes and even higher charges on importing tomato ketchup. Is this deliberately making it difficult for poorer countries to develop?

What causes these variations?

There is no single, simple explanation for global inequalities or social injustices. The many interconnected causes include:

1. Natural environment. Areas of the world like deserts, rainforests and mountains have negative physical factors hindering their development. People living in regions affected by desertification, deforestation or natural disasters are generally poorer. Areas rich in natural resources have a greater chance of developing.

2. Politics. Non-democratic systems may discriminate against particular groups. For example, over a decade after apartheid ended in South Africa, the effects of racist government still show up in extreme variations of wealth between different ethnic groups. Political corruption can also abuse money and power, leading to social injustice. Outcomes of elections everywhere impact the policies governments introduce on equality and justice.

3. History. European countries 'colonised' (took over) countries in Africa, Asia and Latin America and removed natural resources (metals, fuels, wood, minerals) from them. Arguably this damaged development opportunities for those countries. However, from a different perspective, perhaps colonists helped improve the countries they ruled.

4. Economics and trade. Rich regions like North America and Europe use tariffs (import taxes) to protect their economies. Poorer countries argue strongly that this hinders their development. Multi-national companies sometimes exploit poorer countries by paying low wages and abusing workers' rights. Borrowing loans has crippled some nations with debt which stops them investing money into education or health.

5. Social issues. Some cultural traditions disadvantage groups like women. Lack of education or health care can hold back people's potential. The severe HIV/AIDS crisis in Africa is damaging businesses and economies by reducing life expectancy rates and production. Rapid population growth in poorer areas also has an impact.

Are these problems worsened by an unwillingness to face up to responsibility? America, the world's biggest polluter, refuses to sign some crucial environmental treaties. The World Trade Organisation talks in the 'Development Round' ended without progress when the richer 'G7' countries wouldn't agree to change some of their trade practices. 'Intellectual property rights' mean some medicines cannot be sold at affordable prices. Only a minority of people in the developed world buy fair trade products. Are inequalities and injustices a case of caring more for ourselves or our profits than our neighbours?

Consequences

Another international crisis hits the headlines – famine, malnutrition, war, refugees, poverty, human rights violations, environmental destruction. The consequences of global inequalities are widespread. While some individuals resort to violence to be heard, silent millions struggle on in poverty. Individuals lose the freedom to make decisions about their own lives. The world suffers from not helping humanity to develop its full potential. Ultimately the inequalities and injustices can lead to death. Despite our human rights, in practice one life does not seem to be worth the same as another elsewhere in our modern world.

activities

1. Carry out a group role play. Create a 'chat show' sketch debating equality and social justice issues. Characters could include: a Kenyan teenager, a farmer, a politician, a charity worker, a business owner.

2. Use atlases to write a short report comparing statistics and information on rich countries and poor ones.

18. Responding to global inequalities

Participation is the key to changing anything – 'Sympathy is no substitute for action'.

Individuals, societies and governments have different opportunities to promote justice, equality and freedom to make a fairer world possible.

The role of individuals

'He's all talk!' goes the saying. If your only reaction to injustice is 'talk' without action then your response may have limited impact. The fact is, you can make a difference. As another saying goes, 'One person cannot change the world, but you can change the world for one person.' Thousands of individuals make a difference every day by giving donations, campaigning, letter writing, raising awareness, volunteering, voting, buying fair trade produce and making good environmental choices. They are helping to promote a culture of rights, equality and social justice.

Some individuals like Martin Luther King, Gandhi, Nelson Mandela, Aung San Suu Kyi or Mother Teresa may become role models. Film directors, photographers and celebrities can use media publicity effectively, as Princess Diana did for the issues of land mines in Mozambique and AIDS awareness. Some musicians release tracks highlighting injustice like *Where is the Love?* (the Black Eyed Peas No. 1 single in 2003). We have freedom to respond in many ways – others in less fortunate situations may become prisoners of conscience for their efforts.

The role of society

'There is power in numbers', people say. When enough individuals group together to promote global issues, a culture of equality and social justice can develop. NGOs, charities, churches, pressure groups, businesses or community organisations can play a vital role through the following means:

1. Trying to influence government decisions through campaigns, petitions or **lobbying**.

2. Creating publicity for equality, social justice and human rights issues.

3. Helping equality, justice and rights education.

4. Ensuring they are not damaging rights or causing inequality or injustice.

Can business decisions affect rights and equality?

All aspects of society can play a role. For example, the media broadcasts campaigns like Comic Relief. Religious organisations promote global issues in campaigns such as the Trocaire Lenten Campaign or the Tear Fund. Even sporting bodies can make ethical decisions, such as the English cricket team's refusal to play in Zimbabwe; football clubs' stances against sectarianism and racism; or the Olympic Committee's examination of human rights issues when choosing where to hold the Games.

The role of government

Governments can be amongst the worst culprits on issues of human rights, equality and justice. They also, however, have the power to make a big difference. 'Communicate, educate, legislate' sums up much of their role:

1. Communicate. In today's increasingly interdependent world, governments need to communicate with other governments, organisations and individuals to understand global perspectives on issues. This may include listening to advice or criticism, but ultimately good communication will provide better solutions.

2. Educate. Governments can educate their citizens through schools, campaigns and media publicity. The fact that you are studying equality and social justice issues is in many ways the result of a government decision!

3. Legislate. The policies and laws governments create make a difference. Governments must ensure their laws will produce positive global impacts. Actions may include signing agreements on human rights, the environment or trade and taking a positive public stance on relevant issues. Foreign policies on issues like arms exports and import taxes can impact positively or negatively depending on their content.

Can national governments make an international impact?

Global politics – 'Room for improvement?'

Clearly individuals, societies and governments have the potential to make a difference – but are they really doing their best? Many critics argue that rich governments aren't doing enough and are more concerned about winning elections.

It is not simply a case of sending more aid. Developing countries actually receive less in aid and debt relief than they lose through unfair trade practices! Poorer countries are becoming increasingly frustrated by the hard bargaining and pressure of the richer governments at World Trade Talks. The refusal by the richer countries to cut the tariffs, subsidies and quotas which are damaging the poorer countries disgusted African trade ministers so much they walked out of World Trade talks in 1999. After the 2001 talks the poorest countries actually came out worse off in relation to trade. While the EU has recently opened up its markets more, it hasn't made the necessary changes to its agricultural policy. Similarly, America has kept tariffs on steel, cotton and other agricultural imports high and is one of only two countries not to have signed the United Nations Declaration on the Rights of the Child. Despite being the world's largest polluter, the US still won't sign the Kyoto climate agreement. Protests outside the World Trade Organisation meetings are becoming louder and more violent.

activities

1. Make a list of 10 things you could do to promote equality and social justice.

2. What do you think Professor J. Stiglitz (2001 Nobel Prize winner for economic science) meant by this quote:

'The system of global decision-making does not reflect the interests and concerns of the majority of the world's population. ... Rich countries will use their economic muscle to get what they want at the expense of the poor.'

19. Equality and social justice in the media

Media is a general word used to mean TV, radio, newspapers and advertising. The Internet is sometimes also included as a new form of media. In western society, people are aware of the media in everyday life. The media can influence our lives in many different ways, so does its representation of equality and social justice issues also influence us?

The camera never lies – or does it?

Can you believe everything you see on TV? Is America really the way we see it in programmes like *Dawson's Creek*, *Friends* and *ER* and in the Disney World adverts? Is Africa just about famine, poverty, wild animals and blazing sunshine? Is Northern Ireland a constantly violent place with bombs every day? The media influences how we think about places.

Whether we realise it or not, it also influences how we think about people. Are all single, professional women like Bridget Jones? Are all Christians like Harold Bishop from *Neighbours* or Father Ted? Are all Arabs potential Islamic terrorists? How are one-parent families or different ethnic groups represented? No matter what topic you pick, the media is influencing our opinions and knowledge on it. This also applies to our thoughts on equality and social justice issues. Through emphasis and 'hype' the media can make an issue the topic of conversation in canteens and coffee shops across the country. Through bias or targeted advertising it has the power to develop particular viewpoints, trends or crazes. Through omission (leaving out) of certain issues, citizens may know little about some topics or feel they are less important. In the subtle messages we receive through the way that things are presented, stereotypes can be created.

'Tonight's headlines . . . If you are watching this TV at home then you are amongst the richest quarter of the world's population. We remind you again tonight that half the world is still hungry, another 1000 children died today from preventable diseases and conflict, whilst prisoners of conscience continued to be tortured today in over 100 countries. Multi-national companies continue to use child labour and unfair trade practices to give us cheap coffee and sports equipment; and millions of homeless people will sleep on the streets tonight again. So enjoy your dinner and sleep well . . .'

Global village – does the media represent everyone accurately and equally?

A real turn-off?

Many equality and social justice issues are long-term issues with no clear beginnings and endings. The issues are so continuous and widespread around the world that they could fill the news every day of our lives. Poverty, hunger, unemployment, HIV, homelessness, racism, discrimination . . . What do you think would happen to viewing figures or newspaper sales if these topics were prioritised more?

The media is constantly making decisions about what goes in and which stories are left out. After all, they are mainly businesses and need to keep ratings high. Consequently, many equality and social justice issues are omitted because they don't make dramatic enough headlines or because we are only interested briefly before we switch off. For example, there has been a civil war in the Sudan for over 20 years – how often have you heard that reported in the media? Yet when America and Britain invaded Iraq, it filled the news for months. Dramatic natural disasters like hurricanes or earthquakes catch the headlines for a day or two, giving a glimpse of the difficulties of life in other places, but how often do you see headlines about the everyday problems and lifelong struggles of disadvantaged groups or countries?

A positive media role?

On a more positive note, the media can sometimes draw widespread attention to an issue even with only a little coverage. A headline of a flood with images can give a voluntary organisation the initial publicity it needs to launch a successful campaign. NGOs and statutory government agencies can use advertising to catch attention, for example the Department of the Environment's campaign against drink driving or the charity appeals on television. Annual appeals like Children in Need have effectively used the media to focus our thoughts on equality and social justice issues. So the role of the media in such issues can be either positive or negative, but there is no denying it is a powerful tool in influencing people.

activities

1. What is the 'media'?
2. List ways in which the media can help promote equality and social justice issues.
3. 'The media does not represent equality and social justice issues properly.' Do you agree with this statement? Explain your answer.
4. Imagine you work for either an NGO or a statutory government agency. Design a media publicity campaign to draw attention to an issue of equality and social justice.
5. Investigation: On one day, watch the news on the BBC, Channel Four and one other channel, or buy a selection of different newspapers. Make a comparison using the following points.

   • What global issues, equality and social justice issues, or human rights issues are covered?

   • How much time or space is given to other topics like sport, TV, celebrities or weather?

   • Which issues get the main headlines, the front pages or the most airtime?

   • Are there any differences in the viewpoints presented in different papers or on different channels?

   Summarise the main things you have noticed or learnt in your investigation. Can you draw any conclusions about the role of the media in the representation of equality and social justice issues?

20. The impact of human rights standards

Governments and NGOs frequently respond to global problems by producing blueprints explaining how issues should be tackled. These declarations or conventions can also outline a vision of how the world ideally should be. The major documents become accepted human rights standards.

So can they play a role in promoting equality and social justice issues?

Measuring equality, justice and rights through the ECHR

You will already have studied the European Convention on Human Rights (ECHR) in the first section of this textbook (see page 24). Since 1950 it has meant that governments can be taken to court in Strasbourg if individuals feel that their human rights are being broken. However, thinking on human rights has developed considerably since the years after the Second World War when the ECHR and UDHR were written. More recently, the Council of Europe developed two other human rights initiatives based on the ECHR:

1. The European Social Charter (revised 1996) guarantees certain social rights on issues such as employment, education, housing and social security. Collective complaints can be made to the European Committee of Social Rights.

2. The European Convention for the Prevention of Torture (in force since 1989) adds to the ECHR rights for citizens in prison or custody. Expert members of the European Committee for the Prevention of Torture visit places of detention and discuss issues with NGOs to ensure that detainees' rights are upheld.

States which signed up to the Social Charter must report regularly on the progress they have made on putting it into practice. These reports are checked by experts and the states can get a good telling off if progress isn't being made! Similarly, the Committee for the Prevention of Torture insists that governments act on its advice and implement its recommendations. Overall, the ECHR has made many European countries change laws which impacted human rights. For example, Finland changed its law on child custody, while the Netherlands and Austria altered laws on the treatment of mental patients. Sweden updated its law on compulsory religion classes in schools and Belgium changed its laws on homeless people and children born from unmarried parents. Finally, something which you may have strong opinions about – the UK banned corporal punishment in schools!

Consider the local case given opposite.

The development of international human rights law

Despite being the biggest international human rights document, governments cannot be taken to court for abusing the rights in the UDHR. The document is only a declaration or a 'vision' of the rights we should have. It does, however, have power. NGOs can challenge governments or 'shame' them if there is evidence of rights being broken. This can make governments listen. For example, the Brazilian president stated 'We cannot and will not again be a country cited as violent in reports by Amnesty International.' Because it was signed by practically all of the world's countries, the UDHR can be a very useful tool to campaigners hoping to remind governments about rights.

'Second generation rights'

The UDHR focuses mainly on civil and political rights. These are sometimes referred to as 'first generation rights'. In the 1960s, its principles were extended to include some social and economic rights ('second generation rights') and became binding

Disabled man's wait on water supply

The water service may refuse to recognise an appeal court ruling to supply a 79-year-old disabled man with water at his remote Co. Derry home. They have 28 days to decide whether or not to accommodate Claudy man Hugh O'Donnell, who lay undiscovered in a field for three days after breaking his hip, while trekking to his spring well last year ... Mr O'Donnell applied to the Water and Sewerage Service for running water at his life-long home ... but was told it would cost him £11,000 ... He visited Derry Citizens Advice Bureau. Ken Murphy, Tribunal Officer with the CAB, said: 'I was of the firm belief that Mr O'Donnell's human rights had been undermined under various articles in the European Convention on Human Rights.'

© *Belfast Telegraph*, 5 September 2003 (adapted)

---

through two covenants together known as the international Bill of Rights:

1. International Covenant on Civil and Political Rights (1966)
2. International Covenant on Economic, Social and Cultural Rights (1966)

International human rights law has developed since the Second World War mainly in response to particular issues and events. Where there have been seen to be inequalities or social injustices affecting certain groups, new international conventions (agreements) have been written. The first section of this textbook explained how various conventions have been added to international human rights law, including conventions on racial discrimination, discrimination against women, and a convention on the rights of the child (see page 24). All these treaties, and others, together form international human rights law – the human rights standards countries should try to meet.

The 2003 Nobel Peace Prize Winner, Iranian lawyer and women's rights activist Shirin Ebadi. Ebadi campaigned (despite constant death threats) to prove that democratic rights and women's rights are fully possible in Muslim society.

Who monitors international rights?

The individual countries are responsible for ensuring that their citizens have these rights. The UN has the responsibility of checking that countries are implementing the rights they signed up to. Governments must report back every 5 years to relevant UN committees to explain how they are giving their citizens the rights. The committees can also investigate rights issues and pressure governments into changing their laws where necessary. Rights issues relating to equality and social justice on themes like women, poverty, children or education are considered increasingly important in our world.

activities

1. How have human rights developed to include more rights relating to equality and social justice issues?
2. Read the article above. How could a lawyer for Mr O'Donnell use human rights law to argue that he should have a water supply installed for free? (Refer back to page 24 if you need more information on rights.)

45

21. The 'rights' side of the law

Individuals can *promote* human rights, but the government and the justice system are there to *protect* our rights. The law should therefore be designed to protect citizens from discrimination. So what role does the law play in Northern Ireland in protecting us from unfair treatment or social injustices?

The justice system

In simple terms, the justice system is about laws, lawyers, judges, juries and court cases. The justice system doesn't just deal with obvious criminal activities like violent attacks or theft. Many cases involve rights, equality and social justice issues.

'Rights' laws in N.I.

There are many rights and equality laws. For instance the Race Relations Order makes racial discrimination unlawful in issues like employment, education or access to housing and services. Similar laws ban discrimination on the basis of gender, religion and age. They all set clear standards of what is acceptable and what is not. The justice system protects these standards.

Laws are constantly being updated. If a government feels a new law is needed, it suggests it to **parliament** and new legislation can be created. For instance, on 1 January 2000, section 75 Northern Ireland Act became law. It stated that all public authorities have a responsibility to promote equality of opportunity to everyone regardless of religion, politics, race, gender, disability or sexual orientation. New hate law proposals were announced by the government in 2003. These mean that sentences can be increased for cities where sectarianism, racism or bigotry can be proved to be a motive. The biggest single addition to human rights law recently in Northern Ireland has been the introduction of the Human Rights Act.

The Human Rights Act

The Human Rights Act passed by Westminster in 1998 became part of UK law on 2 October 2000. Because the European Court of Human Rights was overworked, signatories of the European Convention on Human Rights were asked to allow human rights cases to be heard in their national courts. The Human Rights Act allowed that to happen in the UK. The Republic of Ireland undertook similar legislation. Previously there was little specific human rights law in the UK and cases were heard in the European Court instead. This was expensive and inconvenient for citizens.

Cases can only be brought against *governments*, not individuals, but everyone benefits from easier access to justice and from the fact that the ECHR has to be taken into account in the way new laws are made or existing ones enforced. It is also hoped that citizens will understand and participate more in human rights issues, confident that their government must consider their rights in all circumstances.

Impact on Northern Ireland

This is the viewpoint of the Northern Ireland Human Rights Commission:

> 'For the first time considering every citizen's human rights will become a central part of our law. Specific rights belonging to all of us will have to be respected, protected and promoted by government ... Crucially, you will now be able to go to a court in Northern Ireland to enforce these rights if necessary.'

Extract from the NIHRC booklet *Human Rights Impact* (www.nihrc.org).

Local citizens have already taken the government (and government organisations) to court and won. UK law may have to be reviewed in areas such as gender and religious discrimination, anti-terrorism and privacy (surveillance, intelligence, communications). Northern Ireland was actually ahead of Great Britain and the Republic of Ireland because all laws made by the **devolved** (regional) **government** since December 1999 had to be in line with the ECHR anyway or else judges could declare the new law illegal!

Does N.I. need a Bill of Rights?

Throughout 'the Troubles' and the peace process, there have been calls for a Northern Ireland Bill of Rights. Under the Belfast (Good Friday) Agreement, the Northern Ireland Human Rights Commission began working to make this a legal reality. However, due to suspensions of devolution this has taken longer than anticipated. The bill remains a 'proposal' and has not yet been finished or given constitutional (legal) status.

Many countries have 'bills' or 'charters' of rights designed to suit the particular unique circumstances in their own state. Issues and priorities may vary from country to country. For example, issues in the

Canadian Charter of Rights (1982) or the South African Bill of Rights (1996) might not have the same relevance or interpretation in Northern Ireland, and crucial issues here might seem irrelevant elsewhere. Whereas international treaties like the UDHR or ECHR cover fundamental human rights, a Northern Ireland Bill of Rights could include more detail or rights specific to circumstances in Northern Ireland.

The Good Friday Agreement says that the Bill of Rights should 'Reflect the principles of mutual respect for the identity and ethos of both communities and parity of esteem.' The rights could include social, economic, civil, cultural or political rights. (See page 26 for more detail.)

activities

1. Name three human rights laws which exist in Northern Ireland.
2. Find out about real cases to do with equality or social justice which have gone to court. You could scan newspapers, search the Internet or invite a lawyer into your class.

Section 75 of the Northern Ireland Act 1998 created new equality laws and rights.

Equality and Social Justice

22. Case study: Amnesty International

'It is better to light a candle than to curse the darkness.' Amnesty International slogan.

Imagine that while watching the news you hear about someone's human rights being broken. How would you react? Would you feel sorry? Tell others? Give money?

In 1961 a lawyer named Peter Benenson read about two Portuguese students arrested in a pub for drinking a toast 'To freedom'. They were sentenced to 7 years' imprisonment. (Portugal was a dictatorship at the time.) Peter acted on this injustice by launching a newspaper appeal to help prisoners of conscience around the world. His efforts resulted in the creation of Amnesty International which today has one million members in 140 countries and is the biggest human rights organisation in the world. It has two aims:

1. To promote general awareness of human rights.
2. To oppose specific abuses of human rights in relation to freedom of conscience and expression, freedom from discrimination and physical and mental integrity (torture and killings).

How does it work?

1. Research – specialists find accurate, detailed and reliable information about human rights abuses and prisoners worldwide.
2. Publicity – awareness is raised about the problem through education, local groups, the media, fundraising and the Internet.
3. Campaigns – human rights activists (members, local groups, you) react to the appeals and do something about the situation. One simple but effective action is to write to the authorities who are abusing human rights and to ask them to stop.
4. Results – governments abusing human rights face increasing pressure and international embarrassment until they hopefully release the prisoners of conscience and stop abusing human rights. Consider this quote from a former torturer in El Salvador: 'If there's lots of pressure, like from Amnesty International, we might pass the political prisoners on to a judge. But if there's no pressure then they're dead.'

activity

Carry out research or invite a representative in to find out what one organisation is doing to help human rights or to tackle issues of inequality and social injustice.

Possible organisations include: Trocaire, Jubilee Action, Save the Children, UNICEF, LASCO, Barnabas Fund, Christian Aid, Casa Alianza, Oxfam, Tear Fund and Amnesty International.

Child labour – what rights should this young girl have?

Torture
When prisoners or others are threatened or inflicted with violence or rape.

Death penalty
When convicted prisoners are executed by the state. This punishment is used disproportionately against ethnic minorities and those too poor to afford a good lawyer.

Disappearances
When authorities abduct or detain people who are never seen again.

AMNESTY INTERNATIONAL

What Amnesty International works to oppose.

Extra-judicial executions
When paramilitary or state organisations murder people.

Prisoners of conscience
When people who have committed no crime are jailed, often for their beliefs or for campaigning for human rights.

Unfair trials
When innocent people are 'set up' or their cases are rigged or based on biased or fabricated evidence.

23. Promoting equality, social justice and human rights in our lifetime

Actions speak louder than words. If this course is only about passing exams then it has failed. Equality and social justice are not things simply to be studied, nor are human rights simply lists of things we can demand. They are values which can impact our lives, our choices and our society.

There are rarely easy answers to difficult questions and people frequently have very different opinions on what the real problems are, never mind how to find solutions! Here are some suggestions:

1. Individuals. Never underestimate the power of one. Many individuals believe in values like 'Love your neighbour as yourself'. Imagine what it would be like if people really practised that! When it comes to equality, social justice and rights, individuals can study, practise and promote the values. If you hear racist or sectarian comments, speak up about it. If you witness or experience social exclusion or discrimination, challenge the perpetrators or support the victims. Use your knowledge of human rights and laws to help prevent discrimination and to promote a fairer society.

2. Society. Groups and organisations in society can promote rights to develop a culture of equality and social justice. On the other hand, if society is indifferent or apathetic, little will change. The media, schools, businesses, churches, NGOs and organisations can speak loudly and act clearly against inequality and discrimination. At the end of the day, democratic governments have to listen to society or they will be voted out.

3. Government. Governments can adopt human rights laws to protect citizens from political, social and economic discrimination. Through legislation, they have the power to insist that citizens and society respect rights. Government organisations can promote equality and social justice by practising human rights values and educating society about rights. Globally, governments can show the

leadership required to make sometimes difficult or unpopular decisions where these are in the wider international interest of equality and social justice.

One world, one chance.

activities

1. Throughout this section on equality and social justice, you will probably have developed your own ideas on issues. Discuss the following as a class:

- What important equality issues exist in Northern Ireland?
- Which social justice issues most affect your area?
- Which global issues made you think?
- Can human rights help promote equality and social justice?

2. Create a display to educate others about equality and social justice.

introduction

The third section of this textbook is about 'Democracy in Action.' Have you ever heard people say 'There's nothing I can do about that!' or 'No one ever listens to me'? This unit will discuss what it means to live in a **democracy**, where as citizens we have the freedom to voice our opinions and influence decisions on issues which are important to us. We will study how countries are governed (run), and especially how the government in Northern Ireland works. Most importantly we will explore how we, as ordinary people, can influence the decisions which our politicians and government make. You will find out how to get *your* voice heard!

24. What is democracy?

Democracy is a concept (idea) rather than a thing. It is to do with how a country (or any group or organisation) is run. Historically the word 'democracy' comes from ancient Greek: *demos* meant common people and *kratos* meant strength or power. Today, a 'democratic' organisation or country is one in which ordinary people have the power to influence how things are run (governed). They can participate in decisions. Often democracy is associated with the idea of freedom and rights. For instance, citizens in a democratic country have the right to vote and are free to voice their opinions.

Bono from U2 makes his voice heard for the Good Friday Agreement. Do you recognise two people on either side of him?

It's simple really . . . Demos is 'people'. Kratos is 'power'. Power to the people.

The word *democracy* comes from ancient Greece.

Two types of democracy

When each person in a group directly casts their own vote, it is called direct democracy. In contrast, representative democracy is when we elect someone else to take decisions on our behalf, such as an MP (Member of Parliament), a local councillor or an MEP (Member of the European Parliament). We may think that democracy is more about politicians, but in some countries such as Switzerland and in a number of states in America, **referenda** and town meetings are frequently used in which the public directly have their say and their governments have to listen!

activities

1. Explain in your own words what democracy means.
2. What are the advantages and disadvantages of the two types of democracy? (Think about when each type would work best.)

Are all societies democratic?

Most countries in the twenty-first century are democratic, but there are still many countries where

Liberté, egalité, fraternité, The French Revolution in 1789 began democracy in France and influenced Europe.

Modern European democracy dates from the French Revolution.

people do not have the same rights and freedoms which we often take for granted. Some states are dictatorships where one leader holds all the power and does what he or she likes! There are also differences between democracies. For example, not all democracies have a president, voting may take place in different ways and elections may be held at different times. Many developing countries became democracies within the last 50 years; other nations have been democratic for centuries.

Government of the people, by the people, for the people shall not perish from the Earth.

Abraham Lincoln, USA 1863.

'Left wing' and 'right wing'

Within democracies, political parties and citizens have wide-ranging views on issues. You may have heard some of the following terms used to describe groups in politics:

Communist   Liberal   Fascist
Socialist   Conservative

Extreme left wing   Centre   Extreme right wing
Left wing   Right wing

After the French Revolution, groups which wanted to change the old system in France sat to the left of the king. Groups which thought more traditionally and were more content with the way things were sat on the king's right-hand side. This is where the terms 'left wing' and 'right wing' originate from. The diagram above is called a 'political spectrum'. The extremist groups at either end don't tend to support democracy and may use violent tactics. The three central groups are found in most democracies and are often represented by different political parties.

How democratic is your school?

Who really holds the power and authority in your school? Who makes the decisions and how can you influence or participate in decision making? In Sweden, some schools allow pupil representatives to take part in interviewing teachers for jobs and promotions! In Northern Ireland, many schools have school councils (a bit like a parliament of pupils) where students can debate their opinions and make sensible suggestions or comments. Discuss how democratic your school is:

- Do you have a school council?
- How are class or school prefects chosen?
- If you have an opinion, are there ways in which you can make your voice heard?
- Do pupils speak up on issues and make reasonable suggestions?
- Do pupils and teachers feel listened to?

activities

1. a) If you were in charge of governing your school, describe what changes you would make.

   b) Would this make it more democratic or more like a dictatorship? Explain your answer.

2. Think about another group which you belong to e.g. your class, youth club or family. How democratic is the group? (Think about how decisions are made, how much people are listened to and how leaders are chosen.)

25. What makes a society democratic?

If democracy means people have the power to influence government, how does that work in practice? What features or characteristics can we look out for to decide whether a society is really democratic?

Elections

Every democratic society gives its citizens the opportunity to voice their opinion and participate by voting in an election. Elections mean the government has to listen to public opinion and can also result in changes in leadership of the country. In democracies, elections must be regular (normally every 3–4 years) and free (there must be a choice of candidates). There are different types of election – general (national), local (for councils) and referenda (votes on a single issue) – and different ways of voting.

Party system

Political parties are organised groups of people who campaign in elections to win seats. They share the same ideas and policies on issues. The four main political parties in Northern Ireland are the DUP, Ulster Unionists, the SDLP and Sinn Fein.

Parliament

Parliament is where politicians discuss and make laws. (The word comes from the French verb *parler* which means to speak.) Frequently there are two parts to a parliament. The United Kingdom has the House of Commons and the House of Lords; Ireland has the Dáil and a Senate; America has a House of Representatives and a Senate. The Northern Ireland Assembly is a regional parliament for Northern Ireland.

Head of state

In a republic, the **head of state** is the president. In a kingdom, the monarch (king/queen) holds the title.

The Republic of Ireland was one of the first countries in the world to have a female president. The Queen of England and the American president are probably among the most famous heads of state.

Prime minister

The prime minister is usually the leader of the political party which wins the most seats in an election. He or she is the leader of parliament and is a very powerful politician.

In what ways do these photographs represent democracy?

The right to criticise!

What might a dictator do if you told him you didn't like his policy on public transport or that his moustache looked strange? One big difference between a democratic society and a non-democratic society is what happens to you if you speak out against government. In a democratic society, you have the right (and the freedom) to protest, voice different opinions and campaign on issues. These rights also mean that the media is free to print or publicise different viewpoints. Many democracies also have a Bill of Rights or follow a code of human rights to protect individuals and minorities. These human rights standards are important in promoting and maintaining democratic societies.

Constitution

A **constitution** is a set of rules about how a country is to be run. It may set down rules about voting, elections, rights and powers. Most democracies have a written constitution – in fact the UK is one of the few states which doesn't.

Power, authority and the rule of law

Power can be positive or negative. A teacher has the power (hopefully!) to make you work in class; a bully has the power to threaten and intimidate you. In a democracy, power is a responsibility which leaders try to use wisely, keeping people's best interests at heart. Most citizens therefore accept their government as the legitimate (rightful) holder of power, even if they don't always agree with its decisions. Similarly, the institutions of law and order, such as the police and courts, are usually reasonably well accepted by most citizens. In other words, the **rule of law** works effectively. Many democracies divide powers between the head of state, the prime minister, the parliament and the courts so that no single area can control everything.

How do power and the rule of law work in a classroom?

Is democracy always best?

A country can set up as a democracy within a couple of years, but it sometimes takes generations to transform society and people into acting and thinking democratically. Northern Ireland is a democratic society, but there are still problems such as violence, sectarianism and unemployment. Some non-democratic rulers in other countries have argued that democracy isn't relevant to all cultures or that it divides society, creating problems and instability. In some developing countries, populations may not be used to it or political and military leaders may be hostile to it. One political analyst wrote 'Ballots [elections] may replace bullets but this does not always broaden popular influence over government. Formal democracy arrives, rather than the substance of a democratic society.' Do you think democracy is important? Is there a difference between a country that says it is democratic and a society which acts democratically?

activities

1. Explain what the following words mean: political party, election, parliament, constitution, head of state.

2. What are the key features of a democratic society? Draw a spider diagram.

3. In a non-democratic society, one person sometimes holds all the power for many years. Why wouldn't this happen in a democracy?

4. Imagine you live in a dictatorship. Design a poster or write a speech to encourage people to campaign for democracy or to publicise which of your human rights are being broken.

26. Democracy and dictatorships

History is full of examples of dictatorships and non-democratic systems. So how did these differ from modern democracy and what impact did they have on individuals and human rights?

Hitler's Germany 1933–1945

Democracy only began in Germany after the First World War. The 1920s, however, were a difficult time in Europe. Non-democratic extremist parties like the Communists and Hitler's Nazi Party gained many supporters who were bitter about the democratic Weimar government's failure to solve social and economic problems in Germany. After a global economic disaster known as the 1929 Wall Street Crash, Germany went bankrupt. Six million people were unemployed and many were hungry and homeless.

Through a mixture of intimidation (threats) by his paramilitary-style army (the SA) and his promises of easy solutions, Hitler was elected chancellor (prime minister) in 1933. He was the first politician to use the media (especially radio) and modern mass campaigns effectively to win support. Once in power, he manipulated the media through censorship (banning certain views) and propaganda (promoting his viewpoints and lies). Indoctrination (brainwashing) of teenagers and children through schools and the Hitler Youth organisations was widespread. The police state also meant that spies and informants regularly sent people to concentration camps. Eventually most Germans – through fear, ignorance or national pride – supported Hitler.

Hitler created laws to destroy democracy gradually. In 1933, the Enabling Act meant he could rule without parliament, and later all political parties apart from the Nazi Party were banned using this law. Trade unions were also outlawed and the Nuremberg Laws in 1935 made Jews in Germany second class citizens who could no longer work in professional jobs, vote, visit certain public places or marry other Germans. Women were told to stick to 'Children, Cooking and Church', and even the churches were frequently influenced or controlled by Nazi officials.

Hitler broke international agreements by developing his army, and after he invaded neighbouring countries in 1939, Britain and France declared war on Germany. Hitler's army committed serious atrocities during the Second World War, breaking humanitarian law. This included the systematic murder of six million Jews and a number of minority groups such as homosexuals, gypsies and disabled people in the Holocaust. It was Hitler's belief that non-Germans and those who were different or troublesome were inferior to his master race of 'Aryan' Germans. In 1945, Hitler committed suicide when Germany lost the Second World War. Germany is now strongly democratic.

Hitler in Nazi Germany.

Milosevic's Yugoslavia

Slobodan Milosevic, leader of the Communist Party, was elected President of Yugoslavia for 13 years. He believed his Serbian people were superior to other ethnic groups and encouraged civil wars in which atrocities, refugees and emigration were common. At Srebrenica in 1995, 7000 Muslims were slaughtered. UN sanctions and NATO air strikes had little impact. Campaigning against Milosevic from inside Yugoslavia was difficult because he controlled the media. However, eventually a huge democratic protest movement and a workers' strike caused the **Belgrade Revolution** in October 2000 which toppled the dictator. In 2001, Milosevic was arrested and tried for 'crimes against humanity' at the UN War Crimes Tribunal in The Hague. In 2003, 'Yugoslavia' was renamed 'The Republic of Serbia and Montenegro'.

Anti-Milosevic protests in Yugoslavia in 2000.

Exposing dictatorships

Many people may have learnt about dictatorships from their history textbooks – Hitler in Germany, Stalin in Russia, Mussolini in Italy or Franco in Spain. Modern dictatorships, however, are often exposed by the media. For example, many of us will have seen news coverage of President Mugabe crushing human rights in Zimbabwe or the case of former Chilean dictator General Pinochet put on trial in Spain. Widespread knowledge of Saddam Hussein's dictatorship in Iraq came through extensive media coverage. The film industry also plays a role. Pol Pot and the Khmer Rouge in Cambodia were exposed in the film *The Killing Fields*, while the apartheid (racist) regime in South Africa came under global pressure after films like *Cry Freedom* and *The Power of One*. Current affairs documentaries frequently expose human rights offenders.

The human rights standards contained in documents like the UDHR, ECHR and the UN Convention on the Rights of the Child are a useful way of measuring democracy. Individuals, voluntary organisations and the media can refer to them in promoting democracy or highlighting where dictatorships have gone wrong. Democratic states also use human rights agreements in monitoring and improving their own systems to maintain healthy democratic societies. For example, the government in Northern Ireland has a responsibility to make sure the principles of the Human Rights Act are applied properly in our society.

activities

1. List the reasons why Hitler's Germany could not be considered a democracy.

2. How did the dictatorships of Hitler and Milosevic break human rights?

3. In what ways can the media:
   a) be abused by dictatorships?
   b) help campaign against dictatorships?

4. How do human rights standards help promote and maintain democratic societies?

5. Use a library, the Internet or a film to research one of the dictatorships mentioned in this section. Explain how it was undemocratic and broke human rights standards.

27. Models of democracy

Whilst democracies have many features in common, they also have differences – there are different models of democracy. In other words, people have their say through elections and political parties and governments will show democratic procedures through parliaments or political leaders, but exactly how this works can vary.

Majority democracy

This model is also known as the **Westminster model**. Found in the UK and New Zealand, it is rare elsewhere. The voting system is 'first-past-the-post' – whoever wins the majority of the votes in an area becomes the Member of Parliament (MP). 'Winner takes all', so to speak, second-place takes nothing. Some critics say that this is unfair. Others argue that it provides a strong and stable political system because usually only two main parties win, creating a strong central government and opposition.

Parliament has two parts (an 'upper' and 'lower' chamber, like the House of Lords and the House of Commons), but the lower chamber is usually far more powerful. There may be no written constitution or clear separation of powers (division of power between the parliament, government and legal system). A lot of work can be achieved in parliament because the government has few problems passing laws due to its majority. It is limited only by self-restraint. However, this perhaps gives the ruling party too much power and may damage overall progress – when another party is voted in, there may be damaging policy changes. The majority model needs a fairly unified society to be a success and rarely works well if there is a sharp division or conflict in society.

Consensus democracy

Consensus democracy is a multi-party system in which parties govern together in a coalition. This model is widespread across Western Europe. Elections are by **proportional representation** (PR). If a party wins 20% of the vote, they win 20% of the seats, i.e. the 'proportion' of the vote they win is equal to the 'representation' they will have in the parliament.

Usually a large number of parties are represented in the parliament. They compromise to ensure they each have some influence in governing. However, governments can be constantly changing if parties disagree on decisions. Critics say that this weakens the government, making decision-making slower and more difficult.

Inside Westminster – parties face each other in confrontation.

Other features of this model include a written constitution, a strong upper chamber in parliament and a 'federal' or decentralised government where power is not all concentrated in one area. The consensus model is often more suited to multi-cultural (mixed) societies so that everyone feels they are being listened to.

It is important to remember that these descriptions are only models. Few countries fit either model exactly.

activities

1. Draw a table to show the similarities and differences between majority and consensus democracy.
2. Which model of democracy do you think would work best in Northern Ireland today? Why?

28. 'The Troubles'

Northern Ireland has a violent history in which the rule of law has sometimes been violated and human rights standards have not always been upheld.

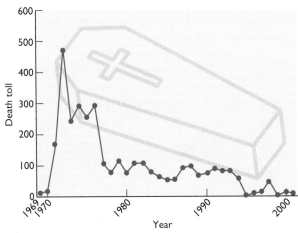

Death toll / Year

Deaths from 'the Troubles' 1969–2001.

activity

Use the information on this page as the basis for class discussion.

- What do you know about the events? Could other events be added in?

- World media represents Northern Ireland as a violent place. Is this a fair representation?

- In what ways have people tried to participate in or influence decision making in Northern Ireland?

- Are there particular human rights issues arising from our recent history?

- Will successful democracy or continued violence impact on your life?

A summary of events from 'the Troubles'

1967	Civil Rights Association formed		Greysteel shootings
1969	People's Democracy March – Burntollet	1994	IRA and Loyalist ceasefires
	Battle of the Bogside	1996	IRA Canary Wharf bomb ended ceasefire
	Widespread sectarian violence – 3500 homeless families		First Drumcree/Garvaghy Road dispute
	Provisional IRA established	1998	Multi-party talks produced 'Good Friday' Agreement.
	O'Neill (PM) resigned		NI referendum showed 71% support
	British troops arrived		First Assembly election
1970	PIRA bombings began		Omagh bomb – 29 dead
1971	UVF revived		First paramilitary prisoners released
	First soldier shot		Nobel Prize for Hume and Trimble
	Internment began	1999	Devolution of power to Stormont
1972	Direct Rule		Patten policing report
	Bloody Sunday – 13 dead	2000	Stormont suspended over decommissioning
	Bloody Friday – 11 dead		Loyalist paramilitary feud
1973	Sunningdale/power-sharing	2001	John Reid became Secretary of State
1974	UWC strike ends power-sharing		Widespread pipe bomb attacks
	Guildford and Birmingham IRA bombs		Real IRA bombs in London
1976	'Peace People' formed		'Holy Cross' school protest
1980–1	Republican hunger strikes		Trimble resigned as First Minister
1984	IRA bombed Conservative Party conference		Serious violence during marching season
1985	Anglo–Irish Agreement signed		One day Assembly suspension – parties discussed
1986	Ulster Says No campaign		difficulties
1987	Enniskillen bomb	2002	Serious violence and murders began anti-sectarian rallies
1988	Hume–Adams talks	2003	May Assembly elections postponed until November
1990–2	Brooke–Mayhew talks	2004	Attempts made to 'kickstart' the peace process again
1993	Downing Street Declaration		

What do local councils do?

Running a country is a lot of work! Decisions can range from dealing with global environmental issues, to providing schools and hospitals, to catching stray dogs, to tackling vandalism. If your bins haven't been emptied for five weeks, it may not help to write to the prime minister. Likewise, your local council may not be able to resolve world ocean pollution!

In order to deal with all the issues, government is divided into layers:

1. Local government (councils) – for everyday local issues.
2. Regional government (e.g. the Northern Ireland Assembly) – for many Northern Ireland issues.
3. National government – for national and international issues.

In Northern Ireland, local councils are responsible for local services. Their work includes providing leisure facilities, waste collections, financial and legal services, maintaining public areas, licensing premises, planning permission, public health and safety, registering marriages, naming streets, running heritage centres, organising local events and festivals, and promoting the area. They co-ordinate campaigns on issues ranging from cycle paths to street drinking to pedestrian zones. Members of local councils are called councillors. Some councils also have a shadow youth council – does yours?

Local council funding

Supplying local services costs money. For example, Derry City Council employs 550 staff in seven departments delivering over 40 services. This costs £18 million annually, so the people of Derry pay rates. Rates are a property tax providing funding for public services. The amount you pay is based on the house you live in. District councils set a 'local rate' to pay for the work they do and the government sets a 'regional rate' to pay for education, housing, social services, water and sewerage, for example.

Councillor profile

Age: Over 21
Address: Lives or works locally
Money: Accesses enough to win elections every four years
Politics: Is usually active in party politics
Council work: Attends council and committee meetings two to three times a month. Takes decisions, presents reports and attends functions.
Pay: Expenses only – no salary!
Aims: Help local area. Possibly progress into regional or national politics.
Other work: Probably has a 'day' job as well.

activity

Carry out a local government investigation. There are 26 local council areas in Northern Ireland. Your task is to investigate and report back on what your local council does. Possible methods of investigation:

- invite a local councillor into your class
- visit your local council offices
- surf your local council's website
- write to your local council.

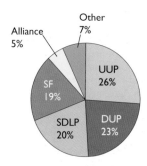

Political party representation in local councils.

What is the Northern Ireland Executive Committee?

First Minister and Deputy First Minister

The First Minister is usually leader of the biggest party in the Assembly. The Deputy is usually leader of the second biggest party. One tends to be from a Unionist party and the other from a Nationalist or Republican party. They 'convene' (call together) and 'preside over' (co-ordinate) meetings and link the Committee to outside organisations.

Minister of Educational Learning
e.g. educational issues ouside schools and universities – like community education

Minister of Education
e.g. schools, 11 plus, further education colleges, universities, teaching issues

Minister of the Environment
e.g. air pollution from traffic or industry, litter and recycling, water quality in rivers and at beaches

Minister of Culture, Arts and Leisure
e.g. developing and promoting festivals, events, music, creative skills, sports facilities, leisure and recreation areas across Northern Ireland

Our Executive Committee will:

1. Discuss and agree on issues, especially issues falling into more than one department (e.g. businesses impacting the environment).
2. Prioritise issues into a programme of government.
3. Recommend a common position on issues if necessary.
4. Produce an annual budget linked to policies and programmes for Assembly approval.

Minister of Regional Development
e.g. ensuring that areas like the North-West or Fermanagh are developed as well as the Greater Belfast area

Minister of Enterprise, Trade and Investment
e.g. grants and schemes for local entrepreneurs, promoting local business abroad, bringing jobs here

Minister of Health, Social Services and Public Safety
e.g. hospitals, doctors, nurses, dentists, local clinics and medical provision, social workers

Minister of Agriculture and Rural Development
e.g. farming, fishing and countryside issues, EU quotas and subsidies

Finance and Personnel Minister
e.g. involvement with how government money is spent in Northern Ireland

Minister of Social Development
e.g. helping people and communities develop skills and take opportunities

Ministers' pledge of office (summary)

I will:
- carry out my duties in good faith.
- be committed to non-violence.
- serve all people in NI equally.
- work with other ministers to prepare a programme of government.
- comply with the Code of Conduct.
- support decisions of the Executive Committee and the Assembly.

Ministers' Code of Conduct (summary)

I will:
- manage public money properly.
- be accountable for meeting my department's targets.
- answer requests for information.
- help promote good community relations.
- not promote my own interests through my job.
- declare any interests which could affect my job.

The **Executive Committee** is the equivalent of the British Cabinet. In the same way as managers lead businesses and make major business decisions, the Executive Committee manages major political decisions and is responsible for carrying out the laws.

It has a First Minister, a Deputy First Minister and ten ministers who are each in charge of a government department. The First Minister and Deputy First Minister are voted in together with cross-community (a majority of Unionist and Nationalist) support. The ten ministerial positions are given out fairly to different political parties under the d'Hondt system which is linked to how many seats each party won in the Assembly elections. A party can change its ministers or refuse the job if it prefers.

The ministers keep in regular contact with their relevant Assembly committees and must stick to the pledge of office and Code of Conduct. They can be sacked by a cross-community Assembly vote if they do not meet their responsibilities.

In protest against the Good Friday Agreement, the DUP didn't attend the meetings up to 2003 and often changed their ministers. The Committee frequently changes, especially after elections.

Who is in office now? Is the executive working or is it suspended?

How does the Northern Ireland Assembly work?

The Assembly is the main **legislative** (law-making) institution in the devolved (regional) government. It was set up as part of the Belfast Agreement (also known as the 'Good Friday Agreement'), and gained its powers in December 1999. It meets at Parliament Buildings in Stormont near Belfast.

Six candidates are elected from 18 **constituencies** (voting areas) across Northern Ireland, making a total of 108 Members of the Local Assembly (MLAs). They meet on Mondays and Tuesdays in the Assembly Chamber for plenary (full) sessions which can involve debates, law making and voting on issues. There is also a ministerial question time. A Speaker (chairperson) controls the meetings and also helps put legislation through the Assembly.

The Assembly has the important job of electing a First Minister and a Deputy First Minister and approving their work. It is also able to express a public response to major issues such as the 'foot and mouth' crisis or 11 September. The Assembly has been suspended on occasions – mainly over the issue of the decommissioning of weapons.

As a devolved government, it has total power over some matters, for example, education, health and agriculture. However, it needs the Secretary of State's consent (see page 67) on issues such as policing and criminal law, and has no control over UK national issues such as defence, **foreign policy** or taxation.

From December 1999–March 2002, the Assembly passed 27 acts (laws) on a range of topics and held debates on issues such as abortion, hospitals, policing, transport, equality, flags and budgets.

The other main work of the Assembly is in committees.

1. Statutory Committees. These 10 committees each shadow a Northern Ireland government department. They have three main powers:
   - Scrutiny – examining and keeping an eye on departments, for example monitoring how money is spent.
   - Policy – they can recommend changes to policies and decisions and can carry out research by asking people or organisations to provide useful information.
   - Initiate legislation – they can start the law-making process by introducing a 'bill' into the Assembly.

2. Standing Committees. These six committees help in the day-to-day running of the Assembly. For example, finance, procedures, Assembly business, audits and public accounts.

3. The Committee of the Centre. This shadows some of the work of the Office of the First Minister and Deputy First Minister.

4. Ad Hoc Committees. These are temporary committees set up for a short time to deal with a particular issue such as flags, proceeds of crime or compensation.

Is the Assembly fair?

The Belfast Agreement wanted to ensure that the Assembly represented everyone.

- MLAs are elected by **single transferable vote** (a type of proportional representation (see page 58)). This means there is always a range of political parties in the Assembly representing Loyalist, Unionist, Nationalist, Republican and 'non-aligned' views.

- Assembly committees and chairs are divided out fairly under the d'Hondt rule.

- Cross-community consent is required on 'key decisions'. This is known as 'parallel consent' or a 'weighted majority'.

- A 'petition of concern' can be presented if 30 MLAs think that an issue should be treated as a 'key decision'.

- All laws made must meet the human rights standards in the European Convention on Human Rights and are 'equality proofed' by the NI Human Rights Commission and the Equality Commission to check that they are fair.

- The public and media can go into the viewing galleries when the Assembly is in plenary session and can see debates live on the Internet or read the official Hansard record of what every MLA says in the Assembly.

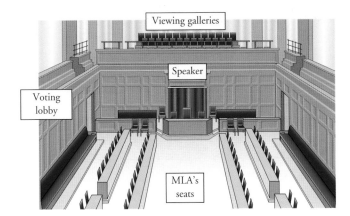

Inside the Assembly chamber.

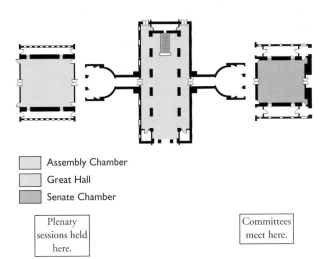

Assembly Chamber
Great Hall
Senate Chamber

Plenary sessions held here.

Committees meet here.

A ground-floor plan of Parliament Buildings.

63

How laws are made

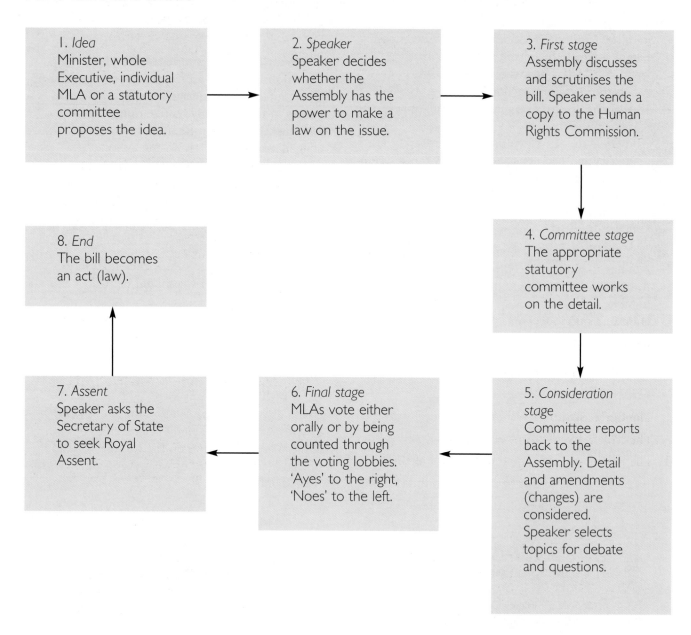

1. *Idea*
Minister, whole Executive, individual MLA or a statutory committee proposes the idea.

2. *Speaker*
Speaker decides whether the Assembly has the power to make a law on the issue.

3. *First stage*
Assembly discusses and scrutinises the bill. Speaker sends a copy to the Human Rights Commission.

4. *Committee stage*
The appropriate statutory committee works on the detail.

5. *Consideration stage*
Committee reports back to the Assembly. Detail and amendments (changes) are considered. Speaker selects topics for debate and questions.

6. *Final stage*
MLAs vote either orally or by being counted through the voting lobbies. 'Ayes' to the right, 'Noes' to the left.

7. *Assent*
Speaker asks the Secretary of State to seek Royal Assent.

8. *End*
The bill becomes an act (law).

activities

Explore the official website of the Northern Ireland Assembly at www.ni-assembly.gov.uk. Try to find the following.

a) The names of six MLAs for your area.

b) The names of the political parties and the number of seats each party has.

c) The weekly diary of an MLA and how much they earn.

d) Up-to-date information about what the Assembly is currently doing.

e) Any four other interesting facts about the Assembly through the virtual tour.

Other institutions created under the Good Friday Agreement

Three further institutions were established under the Good Friday Agreement:

1. The **Civic Forum**
2. The **North-South Ministerial Council**
3. The **British-Irish Council** or **Council of the Isles**

The Civic Forum

Role: To advise the Northern Ireland Executive and be consulted by it on social, economic and cultural issues. The Forum supports democracy by linking wider society to politicians. The idea originally came from the Women's Coalition (a (political party).

Who: 60 unelected members from a range of backgrounds – voluntary, community, business, churches, education, trade unionists, victims, culture, arts, sport, agriculture and six nominees of the First and Deputy First Ministers. Chosen to give a balanced and expert representation of society by gender, religion, geography and age. The Forum is chaired by a local businessman.

Meetings: First met in October 2000. Members serve for three years meeting for approximately six plenary (full) sessions each year. More work however is done in working groups meeting for a few days each month.

Work: There are various ideas. Generally speaking the point is to make use of the wider knowledge and skills in society to help the politicians. This could be done through commenting on assembly legislation, challenging the Assembly or giving it help on issues. The Forum could also tackle issues that the Assembly has no power over, such as parades or punishment beatings or it could look into broad issues such as unemployment or economic strategy and develop its own ideas.

The North-South Ministerial Council

Role: To bring together ministers from the Northern Ireland Assembly and the Irish government to 'develop consultation, co-operation and action within the island of Ireland.'

Who: Ministers with responsibility in the relevant departments from the Northern Ireland Assembly and the Irish government meet. There is also a 'Joint Secretariat' in Armagh made up of civil servants from Northern Ireland and the Republic of Ireland. They help organise meetings and business.

Meetings: First met in December 1999. Has approximately two plenary meetings and four sectoral (area) meetings annually.

Work: It is designed to work on areas 'of mutual [common] interest' and to develop common policies where everyone on the island could benefit.

The British-Irish Council (Council of the Isles)

Role: To promote harmonious and mutually beneficial development of the totality of relationships among the peoples of these islands. In other words, to try to make sure that people on all the islands in the British Isles get on well together.

Who: The Council is attended by government ministers from London and Dublin, ministers from the devolved parliaments in Northern Ireland, Scotland and Wales, and representatives from the Isle of Man, Guernsey and Jersey.

Meetings: First met in December 1999. Summit meetings involving the Prime Ministers and leaders usually take place two times a year. Sectoral meetings also take place involving officials and ministers from the various member countries.

Work: It is a forum where politicians can consult with one another, co-operate and exchange views. Usual work includes agriculture, health, regional issues, inter-parliamentary links, tourism, energy, culture, education, sport, prisons and EU issues.

activities

1. Is the Civic Forum a waste of time?

   Should the North–South Ministerial Council exist?

   Is the Council of the Isles really worth the money and effort?

   What is your opinion on the three institutions?

2. As a class, pick a well-known topic currently in the Northern Ireland news. Set up a mock meeting of the Civic Forum to debate the issue.

Northern Ireland, Great Britain and the Republic

A map of the British Isles and the Channel Islands.

Officially part of the UK, yet geographically on the island of Ireland, Northern Ireland has links with both Great Britain and the Republic. The European Union, North–South Ministerial Council and the Council of the Isles also contribute.

Westminster

At least every 5 years, Northern Ireland elects 18 MPs to the House of Commons. The Ulster Unionists, Democratic Unionists, SDLP and Sinn Fein each have MPs, although Sinn Fein representatives do not actually sit in the Commons because they object to the oath of allegiance which MPs must swear. Election results

Which of the issues discussed by the British-Irish Council are important to you?

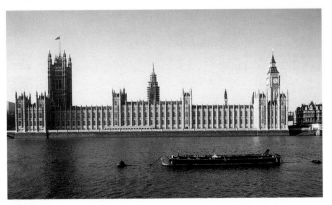
Westminster.

usually return about 11 Unionists and seven Nationalists (most of whom are also MLAs and sometimes MEPs!). The Unionists tend to vote with the Conservative Party, the SDLP with the Labour Party.

The Secretary of State

Do you recognise these names – Mo Mowlam, Peter Mandelson, John Reid and Paul Murphy? They have all been Secretary of State for Northern Ireland. It is a British cabinet job so its holder often changes in cabinet 'reshuffles'. The Secretary of State, with the support of the Northern Ireland Office (NIO), is the British government's representative in Northern Ireland. He or she has responsibility for 'reserved matters' which are not under the devolved government's control. These include constitutional and security issues such as policing, criminal justice, law and order, and prisons. If Stormont is suspended, the Secretary of State and the NIO assume responsibility for all government work. Arguably this is a disadvantage, because it means that decisions aren't made by local people. The Secretary of State also voices Northern Ireland issues in Westminster and ensures that central government policies are carried out locally.

The British monarchy

The Queen is head of the government, the judiciary and the armed forces. Royal family members sometimes visit Northern Ireland – events which symbolise to many Unionists an important link with Great Britain.

The budget

Unlike the Scottish Parliament, the Northern Ireland Assembly has no tax-raising powers – it depends on Westminster for cash! Arguably without the link to Britain, Northern Ireland might have less money for services like schools, hospitals and roads.

The prime ministers

Successive British prime ministers and Taoisigh (Irish prime ministers, singular **Taoiseach**) have led the way in improving relationships between Great Britain, Ireland and Northern Ireland. Important prime ministerial announcements have driven the peace process forward at crucial times.

activities

1. Find out the answers to the following questions:
   a) Who is your MP?
   b) Who are the current 18 MPs for Northern Ireland?
   (Try surfing the Internet or writing to Parliament to find out.)
2. Why do you think 'reserved matters' remained the responsibility of Westminster?

30. The EU and Northern Ireland

After the two World Wars, European politicians hoped to promote peace and democracy by developing economic and political links. In 1952 they began what is now known as the European Union (EU). The UK and Ireland joined in 1973.

The Treaty of Amsterdam (1997) updated how the EU works. It has no powers over national issues like income tax, education or social security. Instead it concentrates on issues needing international co-operation like the environment, foreign aid and science. With 450 million citizens, 25 countries and the world's largest multi-national parliament (consensus model), the EU is a powerful democratic association. Ten of the 25 countries (from Central Europe and the Mediterranean) joined on 1 May 2004 in a major expansion.

The main EU institutions

The main EU institutions are located in Brussels, Strasbourg and Luxembourg. They are:

European Parliament
Legislature (law-making body). Controls budget. Made up of 622 MEPs elected every 5 years, including three from Northern Ireland.

European Commission
'The heart of Europe'. Proposes ideas for laws and organises big initiatives like the introduction of the Euro. Guardian of the treaties (checks members keep their promises!).

Council of the European Union
Executive body – carries out the laws. Rotates the presidency every 6 months. Runs common security and foreign policies.

What impact does the EU have on Northern Ireland?

◆ 11% of the EU budget goes through regional funds to disadvantaged areas – Northern Ireland received 300 million Euros for peace projects from 1995–1999.

◆ 50% of the budget is spent on CAP (Common Agricultural Policy) to help farmers and consumers. To control overproduction it sets quotas (limits) and helps the environment by encouraging new crops, setting land aside, forestry and avoidance of chemicals.

◆ The Common Fisheries Policy stops overfishing. It sets quotas, limits boats or bans fishing in protected areas. Ports are developed and fishing communities retrained into other jobs like tourism.

◆ The EU works with other organisations to send humanitarian aid to needy countries.

◆ Trans-European transport networks paid for by the EU include rail links between Cork and Belfast, roads through Ireland and the UK and ferry links to Scotland and Wales.

◆ EU laws on recycling, rivers, beaches, air, forests, pollution, energy efficiency and wildlife help the environment. Building projects now need to be checked to see if they damage the environment before being granted permission to go ahead.

activities

1. Discuss whether the EU has a positive or negative impact on Northern Ireland.
2. Write to the European Commission (Windsor House, 9/15 Bedford Street, Belfast) or explore www.europarl.eu.int to research what has recently been discussed by the EU.

31. The Council of Europe

Headquarters of the Council of Europe.

To tackle problems in European society like discrimination, crime, intolerance, AIDS and environmental issues.

To protect human rights.

To promote Europe's cultural diversity.

Aims of the Council of Europe

To protect the Rule of Law.

To support political and legal reforms and improve democracy.

To protect democracy.

To help guarantee fundamental freedoms for citizens.

Europe's conscience

The Council of Europe was set up in 1949 and is sometimes nicknamed 'Europe's conscience' by its 45 member states. It is not the same as the European Union, but it is an intergovernmental organisation based in Strasbourg (France). So what does it do and how does it impact governments or individuals?

What does it do?

Any European state accepting the aims (see page 69) can join. The Council of Europe deals with any European issues apart from defence, but is mainly known for its work on cultural, environmental, ethical and human rights issues. Notably it created the European Convention on Human Rights which allows human rights cases to be brought before the European Court of Human Rights.

Unlike the EU, the Council of Europe cannot make or enforce laws, but it does influence EU legislation and helps young democracies (like those in Eastern Europe) to develop. It also creates 'conventions' (guideline agreements or 'blueprints') which member states can decide to adopt (ratify) in their own countries. For example, the United Kingdom adopted the ECHR into its laws in the Human Rights Act and now has a responsibility to ensure that the human rights of its citizens are properly respected.

How is it run?

The Council of Europe is directed by its elected Secretary General and also has a Committee of Ministers and a Parliamentary Assembly whose members are appointed by national parliaments. Ordinary people also have a say – the Congress of Local and Regional Authorities of Europe allows local and regional authorities to participate directly and over 350 NGOs are officially recognised as partners who are consulted on issues.

activities

1. Why do you think the Council of Europe is nicknamed 'Europe's conscience'?

2. Debate or discuss these issues from the Council of Europe:

   • The death penalty: The Council of Europe says the death penalty should be banned in all circumstances. Do you agree?

   • Euthanasia: Diane Pretty lost her case in 2002 for 'the right to die with dignity'. Do you agree with the decision of the European Court of Human Rights?

   • Sport: Violence, discrimination, drugs and racism are issues in sport. Can sport help promote tolerance?

   • Citizenship education: The Council of Europe's 'millennium vision' included education for democracy and cultural diversity. Should everyone be educated in citizenship?

   • Media: Is freedom of expression and information important and can the media help democracy?

3. What other issues do you think are currently important?

32. The United Nations

Over 190 nations (practically all that exist worldwide) are members of the UN. Based in New York, it was set up after the horrors of the Second World War as an attempt to preserve peace through partnership. Unlike governments, it doesn't make or enforce laws, but its General Assembly is like a 'parliament of nations'. World issues are debated and wealthy, poor, big and small states all have their say. UN recommendations are like global opinion polls and carry a lot of moral authority. In a sense, the United Nations is the 'biggest club in the world'.

The UN also has a Secretary General who co-ordinates the organisation (especially in peacemaking) and a Security Council which aims to keep international peace and security. The five permanent members of the Security Council – China, France, Russia, the UK and the USA – play a powerful role in times of international crisis or war. The Economic and Social Council helps development and social issues and works with NGOs, while the International Court of Justice or 'World Court' judges on disputes between countries.

What does the UN do?

A simple way of summarising the role of the UN is that it gives the world PRIDE:

P = Peace. Peacemaking by helping solve disputes peacefully. Peacekeeping by sending international security forces to help in conflict areas. Peacebuilding by tackling the root causes of conflict, and disarmament by destroying or outlawing the worst weapons.

R = Rights. Creating human rights documents such as the UDHR in 1948 (see page 20). Ensuring rights are implemented through monitoring countries and helping states to improve. Protecting and promoting human rights including economic and social development rights.

I = International law. The UN helps to write the drafts (conventions) for better international laws which countries then agree to. For example, laws on trade, the environment and terrorism.

D = Development. The majority of the UN's work is in improving development through economic, social and environmental progress.

E = Emergency assistance. The UN provides emergency or 'humanitarian' assistance after natural or man-made disasters. Working with NGOs it provides medicine, shelter and food to suffering people like refugees. UNICEF is among the best known UN agencies.

activity

Find out where the UN is currently working through the media or by looking at www.un.org

UN Charter:

1. Keeping international peace and security.
2. Developing friendly relations among nations.
3. Co-operating in solving international problems and promoting respect for human rights.
4. Harmonising the actions of nations.

Peacekeeping and human rights.

Millennium Declaration 2000

We, the UN member states, agree to aim for specific goals in:
1. Peace, security and disarmament.
2. Development and wiping out poverty.
3. Environmental protection rights.
4. Human rights and democracy.
5. Protecting the vulnerable.
6. Helping Africa.
7. Strengthening the U.N

33. How can you influence political decisions?

Who can vote?

Until 1918 only wealthy, upper class men in the UK could vote. Suffragettes (women's rights campaigners) campaigned through lobbying, **civil disobedience** and **direct action** until women won the vote in 1918. They (and others worldwide today) saw the vote as an important right worth fighting for. Since 1969 the voting age has been 18 for all adults equally in the UK. This is called universal suffrage. However, elderly, unemployed, poor and young people are less likely to vote and turnout at elections is falling in the UK as a whole. To vote, you must be registered in your local **constituency** and be able to produce photographic ID.

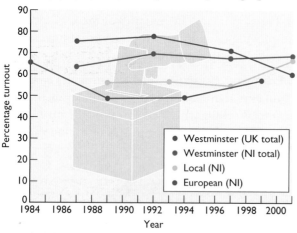

Election turnout.

activities

1. What does the graph above show about election turnout?

2. Tactical voting – is it always best to vote for your favourite candidate?

3. Abstention – if more people voted, what difference might it make?

4. Conduct a poll (survey) to research who votes. What reasons do people have for voting or abstaining? Should voting be compulsory or allowed via the Internet? Should the voting age be lowered?

Types of voting system

1. First past the post

Literally 'X' marks the spot!

Used for Westminster elections. The candidate with the most votes in a constituency wins – the rest get nothing.

2. Single transferable vote (STV)

As easy as, one, two, three!

Voters number the candidates in order of preference. This type of PR system is used for local Northern Ireland elections, Assembly elections and European elections. The constituency area is wider – perhaps three people will be elected for one larger area. Counting occurs in rounds. Candidates must reach a quota (set number) of votes.

Step 1 – The first preferences (number 1 votes) are counted. Any candidates reaching the quota are elected. The bottom candidate is eliminated.

Step 2 – The second preferences of the eliminated or elected candidates are counted out to remaining parties. Candidates now reaching the quota are elected. The bottom candidate is eliminated.

Step 3 – This continues until all the seats are filled.

3. Referendum

A 'yes' or 'no' vote on an issue. The electorate answers a specific question on a topic. The vote on the Agreement is a good example of this (over 80% of voters turned out!). Should we have a referendum on joining the Euro?

What do political parties do?

In a representative democracy, citizens vote for politicians to speak up on their behalf. Northern Ireland has over 10 political parties. Can you recognise any from the images below? Parties here fall into three main groups – Unionist (including Loyalist), non-aligned and Nationalist (including Republican). Unionist parties want to keep the union (link) with Great Britain and are normally voted for by Protestants. Nationalist parties identify more with the nation of Ireland and are mainly supported by

Catholics. Non-aligned parties take a centre or neutral position and have members from all communities.

However it is not just the constitutional position of Northern Ireland that the electorate votes about. The parties have policies on issues like hospitals, education, benefits, taxes, Europe, transport, economy and the environment. These are set out in their **manifesto**. Nationalist parties are frequently more socialist (left wing) than the more conservative Unionist group, although there are exceptions. Party policies may vary depending on whether the party thinks traditionally and is reasonably happy with existing practices or whether they are more radical and want big changes. Who you vote for can therefore influence important issues for you. If you feel very strongly about politics, you could become a member of a political party and help their campaigns, as well as voting.

Logos of some of the Northern Irish political parties.

1. Which voting system (see page 72) is fairest? Which is easiest?

   Try the systems in class to decide on favourite music or football teams.

2. Construct a table with headings for Unionist, Non-aligned and Nationalist. Place the following parties under the correct heading: Sinn Fein, The Green Party, Ulster Unionist Party, Democratic Unionist Party, Women's Coalition, The Alliance Party, PUP, UKUP, Natural Law Party.

3. Carry out some research. What different policies do parties have on issues important to you or your family? Which party do you prefer?

As well as the formal politics of voting, referenda and political parties, there are less formal ways of influencing government decisions. In the twenty-first century, more citizens are members of pressure groups than political parties.

What are pressure groups?

Pressure groups are also known as 'interest groups' or 'non-governmental organisations' (NGOs). They try to influence government. Normally they form around a single issue such as the environment, workers' rights or anti-war campaigns. Amnesty International (see page 48) and Greenpeace are well-known examples.

What tactics do they use?

1. Lobbying – The entrance hall area inside the Houses of Parliament is called the 'Central Lobby'. This is where people traditionally meet MPs to discuss views on issues. Lobbying involves meeting or contacting politicians to express opinions and trying to persuade them to consider your cause. Letters, petitions and meetings are common types of lobbying. Some pressure groups employ professional lobbyists, and lobbying can sometimes successfully influence laws.

2. Civil disobedience – When an individual or group breaks the law in a non-violent protest, it is known as civil disobedience. Examples include stopping a road construction by tunnelling underground or being chained to a tree. Refusing to pay taxes to highlight a cause is another tactic.

3. Direct action – This more extreme form of protest uses violent tactics. Animal rights campaigners, for instance, have sometimes fire-bombed animal research labs. Sabotage (cutting phone, electricity or water supplies, for example) is another direct action tactic. These extreme tactics do gain high publicity, but may have a negative impact on the lives or opinions of ordinary citizens, so the actions can 'backfire'.

4. Media publicity – Governments and politicians use the media constantly to try to influence us. They employ 'spin doctors' to twist news to their benefit or to time when stories are released. If they can do that, why shouldn't we? Media publicity generally boosts campaigns and protests. Pressure groups use adverts, press releases and media stunts to attract maximum attention to their cause.

1. The events opposite are real reports taken from the Northern Ireland media.

   a) What type of tactics do they represent?

   b) What impacts might they have had?

   c) Which issues do you feel most or least strongly about?

2. Discuss as a class:

   a) Have you ever campaigned?

   b) Do you have opinions on issues that you would like politicians to listen to?

   c) How could you campaign to achieve your goal?

   Why not lobby the relevant authorities and see if you receive a response?

The mobile phone mast after being chopped down.

Mobile phone mast is cut down in cancer alert (17 December 2002)

A 150-foot-high mobile phone mast which local residents thought was causing cancer has been cut down. In an operation which included negotiating a 15-foot-high electrified fence, protesters used an angle grinder to cut through the mast's four legs.

Thousands take to Ulster's streets in call for peace (19 January 2002)

Tens of thousands of people took to the streets of Northern Ireland yesterday in one of the biggest peace demonstrations the province has ever seen. In the driving rain, trade unionists addressing rallies called for an end to all sectarian violence and harassment.

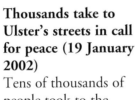

Protest at sea.

Nuclear freighters greeted by protest flotilla (17 September 2002)

Environmental campaigners staged a protest yesterday against two nuclear freighters that entered the Irish Sea carrying a cargo of rejected plutonium fuel. The peaceful protest, led by Greenpeace, spread out across the Irish Sea to intercept the ships and highlight the dangers of nuclear material.

Don't pay TV licence fee, campaigners urge viewers (8 November 2002)

A former Soviet dissident launched a campaign of civil disobedience yesterday by urging television viewers not to pay their licence fee. Vladimir Bukovsky, 60, who alleges that the BBC is biased, said earlier this week that he was willing to go to jail for refusing to pay the fee.

The countryside comes to Dublin!

Tractors mass in Dublin protest (11 January 2003)

Hundreds of farmers drove their tractors into the centre of Dublin yesterday at the climax of a week-long campaign against falling farm incomes.

Protest has rattled number 10, say march organisers (17 February 2003)

Organisers of the biggest public demonstration in British history yesterday criticised the Government's response to the protests across the world against war in Iraq.

Militant group declares 'war' on hunt ban (17 November 2002)

Militant hunt supporters are threatening to sabotage essential services, including electricity pylons, gas supplies and food deliveries, in reaction to the Government's decision to introduce a bill that would ban foxhunting.

Angry scenes over casualty closure (17 August 1999)

Officials from a Northern Ireland health board were heckled at a public meeting over plans to close the accident and emergency department of a hospital.

Lobbyists outside 10 Downing Street.

Families lobby for tougher sentences (23 January 2003)

Campaigners against car crime in Northern Ireland have handed in a letter to Prime Minister Tony Blair calling for tougher sentences for offenders. The group, Families Bereaved Through Car Crime, will share a platform with senior Northern Ireland politicians at Westminster.

75

Glossary

Words given in **bold** text appear elsewhere in the glossary.

Asylum seeker A person who has fled their own country and is seeking 'refugee status' in a new country.

Belgrade Revolution When events in Serbia in 2000 overturned the Milosevic dictatorship peacefully.

Belief Something that is regarded as important and worthwhile.

Biculture A situation where there are only two **cultures**.

Bigotry Attitudes or behaviour which demonstrate intolerance and **prejudice**.

Bill of Rights A document of human rights specific to a particular country.

Blasphemy laws Crimes committed if a person insults or offends the Christian religion.

British–Irish Council See entry under **Council of the Isles**.

Civic Forum A group of 60 citizens from Northern Ireland formed to help involve ordinary people more in politics.

Civil disobedience Breaking the law in non-violent protest.

Civil society A system of cultural patterns and institutions providing protection and security for all its members.

Cohesion The act of uniting. Agreement between individuals or groups.

Collective rights The fact that all individuals in society have the same rights.

Consensus A multi-party system where parties elected by **proportional representation** govern together in a coalition.

Constituency A voting area or region.

Constitution A set of rules about how a country is run.

Council of the Isles An institution which organises meetings for politicians from the UK, Ireland and the Channel Islands.

Councillors Elected local officials responsible for local services.

Culture The language, **beliefs**, **values**, **norms**, **customs**, **roles**, knowledge and skills which combine to make up the 'way of life' of any society.

Cultural relativism The belief that no **culture** is superior to another.

Custom A long-established tradition of a society collectively.

Decommissioning Putting weapons permanently beyond use. 'Getting rid of guns.'

Democracy A political system in which people can vote and influence how their country is run.

Democratic tactics Peaceful, legal tactics to bring about change. Also called 'constitutional tactics'.

Devolved government The regional government for Northern Ireland.

Devolved institutions Regional political bodies including the NI Assembly and the executive committee, the Scottish Parliament and the Welsh Assembly.

Discrimination The unfair treatment of others where the action is based on **prejudice**.

Direct action Extreme protest tactics often using violence.

Domestic law A government's policies about issues inside its own country.

Equality Where individuals and groups are treated equally and fairly and everyone has the same opportunities.

European Convention on Human Rights A human rights document with legal status in many European countries.

Exclusion The act of leaving out, rejecting or refusing to consider.

Executive Committee The group of top politicians from different political parties who make the important decisions. They are each 'ministers' responsible for a government department.

Extra-judicial execution When paramilitary or state organisations murder people without trial.

Foreign policy A government's international policies towards other countries and international issues.

Gender The social and cultural differences between men and women.

Genocide The policy of deliberately killing a nationality or ethnic group.

Harmony Agreement in action, feeling or opinion between individuals or groups.

Head of state
The king/queen or president of a country.

Human Rights Act
The document which meant that the European Convention on Human Rights became part of UK law and ensured human rights cases could be heard in UK courts.

Human rights standards
Human rights values outlined in many conventions and declarations on human rights.

Identity The individual characteristics by which a person is recognised.

Inclusion The act of including.

Inequality Where people are not all treated equally or fairly.

Legislation A document discussed in **parliament** which becomes law if parliament agrees.

Lobbying Trying to influence politicians' opinions on issues.

Manifesto A document in which a political party sets out its aims, ideas and policies.

Multiple identities
The fact that individuals may have a number of characteristics which allows them to be recognised as having more than one **identity**.

NGO
A 'non-governmental organisation'. Also known as interest groups or pressure groups.

Norm A specific guideline for behaviour in particular circumstances.

North–South Ministerial Council
Groupings of ministers from the Irish and Northern Irish governments who consult and co-operate on areas of common interest.

Parliament A legislative (law-making) institution.

Peer group A group sharing the same social position in society.

Prejudice Intolerance or dislike for people of a particular race, religion etc.

Prisoner of conscience
Person imprisoned solely because of their beliefs or because of who they are.

Proportional representation (PR)
A voting system in which political parties receive a percentage of seats in **parliament** directly equal to the percentage of votes they win. For example, 20% of the vote = 20% of the seats.

Race The classification of humans into different groups according to physical characteristics, like skin colour.

Racial discrimination
When someone is at a disadvantage or treated differently because of their **race**.

Racial prejudice
When an individual believes that some 'races' are superior to others.

Reconcile When friendly relations are re-established between two or more people.

Referendum
When citizens are given the opportunity to vote 'yes' or 'no' on an issue.

Revolutionary tactics
When violence is used to try to bring about change.

Role The pattern of behaviour which is expected from particular individuals in society.

Rule of law A democratic society in which citizens are generally peaceful and under control is said to respect the 'rule of law'.

Scapegoat When a person or group is blamed for something that is not their fault.

Sectarian The narrow-minded promotion of the interests of one particular sect.

Sectarianism
Discrimination, **prejudice** or unfair treatment based on a person's religion.

Segregation The practice or policy of creating separate facilities within the same society for the use of a minority group.

Sex The biological differences between males and females.

Single transferable vote (STV) The type of **proportional representation** used in some Northern Ireland elections. Voters number their preferences 1st, 2nd, 3rd etc.

Socialisation The process by which we learn the **norms**, **values** and **roles** expected of us.

Social solidarity
The feelings of identification and mutual interest by a social group.

Stereotype A generalised, over-simplified view of the features of a social group.

Taoiseach The Irish prime minister.

The Troubles A term commonly used in Northern Ireland to describe the conflict between the two opposing traditions since 1969.

Transgender
Those individuals who belong to one particular **gender** group, for example, masculine, but who dress and act like those who belong to the other gender group, in this case, the feminine gender group.

Value A **belief** that underlines **norms**.

Value consensus
The general agreement by all members about what things are important and worthwhile in society.

Westminster model
A system of majority **democracy** with two main political parties.

White supremacy
The promotion of the white **race** as superior at the expense of all others.

77

Useful addresses and websites

Amnesty International Northern Ireland
397 Ormeau Road
Belfast
BT7 3GP
Tel: 028 90 643 000
Email: nireland@amnesty.org.uk
Website: www.amnesty.org.uk

The Northern Ireland Assembly
Parliament Buildings
Stormont
Belfast
BT4 3XX
Tel: 028 90 521 333
Email: info.office@niassembly.gov.uk
Website: www.ni-assembly.gov.uk

The Civic Forum
c/o The Civic Forum Secretariat
Room E5.03
Castle Buildings
Stormont Estate
Belfast
BT4 3SR
Tel: 028 90 523 113
Email: secretariat@civicforum-ni.org
Website: www.civicforum-ni.org

The Northern Ireland Human Rights Commission
Temple Court
39 North Street
Belfast
BT1 1NA
Tel: 028 90 243 987
Email: nihrc@belfast.org.uk
Website: www.nihrc.org

The Equality Commission for Northern Ireland
Equality House
7–9 Shaftesbury Square
Belfast
BT2 7DP
Tel: 028 90 500 600
Email: information@equalityni.org
Website: www.equalityni.org

Community Relations Council
6 Murray Street
Belfast
BT1 6DN
Tel: 028 90 227 500
Email: info@community-relations.org.uk
Website: www.community-relations.org.uk

Incore
Aberfoyle House,
Northland Road,
Londonderry,
BT48 7JA,
Tel: 028 7137 5500
Email: incore@incore.ulst.ac.uk
Website: www.incore.ulster.ac.uk

Some of the main Northern Irish political parties

Democratic Unionist Party
91 Dundela Avenue
Belfast
Northern Ireland
BT4 3BU
Website: www.dup.org.uk

Ulster Unionist Party
Cunningham House
429 Holywood Road
Belfast
BT4 2LN
Tel: 028 90 765 500
Email: uup@uup.org
Website: www.uup.org

SDLP
Head Office
121 Ormeau Road
Belfast
BT7 1SH
Tel: 028 90 247 700
Email: sdlp@indigo.ie
Website: www.sdlp.ie

Sinn Fein
53 Falls Road
Belfast, BT12 4PD
Tel: 028 90 223 000
Email: sfadmin@eircom.net
Website: www.sinnfein.iet

Alliance Party
88 University Street
Belfast
BT7 1HE
Tel: 028 90 324 274
Email: alliance@allianceparty.org
Website: www.allianceparty.org

Women's Coalition
50 University Street
Belfast
BT7 1HB
Tel: 028 90 233 100
Email: info@niwc.org
Website: www.niwc.org

Green Party
The Green Party
1 Burnside Road
Dunadry,
Antrim,
BT41 2HZ
Tel: 028 94 432 026
Email: vote@greens-in.org
Website: www.greens-in.org

Progressive Unionist Party
182 Shankill Road

Belfast
BT13 2BH
Tel: 028 90 326 233
Email: central@pup-ni.org.uk
Website: www.pup-ni.org.uk

Some general websites

Save the Children
www.savethechildren.org

UNICEF
www.unicef.org

Oxfam
www.oxfam.org

Barnardos
www.barnardos.org

Christian Aid
www.christianaid.org.uk

Disability Action
www.disabilityaction.org

Trócaire
www.trocaire.org

Tear Fund
www.tearfund.org

Irish News
www.irishnews.co.uk

Belfast Telegraph
www.belfast/telegraph.co.uk

News Letter
www.newsletter.co.uk

Index